# Legalines™

Editorial Advisors:
**Gloria A. Aluise**
Attorney at Law
**Jonathan Neville**
Attorney at Law
**Robert A. Wyler**
Attorney at Law

Authors:
**Gloria A. Aluise**
Attorney at Law
**David H. Barber**
Attorney at Law
**Daniel O. Bernstine**
Attorney at Law
**D. Steven Brewster**
C.P.A.
**Roy L. Brooks**
Professor of Law
**Frank L. Bruno**
Attorney at Law
**Scott M. Burbank**
C.P.A.
**Jonathan C. Carlson**
Professor of Law
**Charles N. Carnes**
Professor of Law
**Paul S. Dempsey**
Professor of Law
**Jerome A. Hoffman**
Professor of Law
**Mark R. Lee**
Professor of Law
**Jonathan Neville**
Attorney at Law
**Laurence C. Nolan**
Professor of Law
**Arpiar Saunders**
Attorney at Law
**Robert A. Wyler**
Attorney at Law

*604 – 623 not covered*

# ADMINISTRATIVE LAW

## Adaptable to Fifth Edition of Schwartz Casebook

By Paul S. Dempsey
Professor of Law

THE
**barbri®**
GROUP

A THOMSON COMPANY

EDITORIAL OFFICES: 111 W. Jackson Blvd., 7th Floor, Chicago, IL 60604
REGIONAL OFFICES: Chicago, Dallas, Los Angeles, New York, Washington, D.C.

SERIES EDITOR
Angel M. Murphy, J.D.
Attorney at Law

PRODUCTION MANAGER
Elizabeth G. Duke

FIRST PRINTING—2003

# Legalines™

# SHORT SUMMARY OF CONTENTS

# TABLE OF CONTENTS AND SHORT REVIEW OUTLINE

# I. INTRODUCTION: ADMINISTRATIVE AGENCIES AND ADMINISTRATIVE LAW

## A. WHAT IS ADMINISTRATIVE LAW?

Administrative Law consists of the procedural and substantive law of governmental agencies. The course in Administrative Law focuses on the generic processes and procedures of all administrative agencies, federal and state. Hence, the substantive law produced by administrative agencies is covered in other courses (*e.g.,* the substantive law created, defined, and interpreted by the National Labor Relations Board, an administrative agency, is examined in Labor Law; the substantive law of the Internal Revenue Service of the Treasury Department is covered in Tax Law). The substantive law of administrative agencies is discussed in this course for illustrative purposes only. The course in Administrative Law reviews how substantive authority is delegated to administrative agencies, the procedural limitations upon the exercise of such authority, and remedies against unlawful agency action.

### 1. Sources of Administrative Law.

  a. **Federal Administrative Procedure Act.** The principal procedural foundation of federal agencies is the Administrative Procedure Act ("APA"), promulgated in 1946.

  b. **Model State APA.** Corresponding state legislation has been enacted in almost all states, most of which has been patterned after the Model State APA.

  c. **Judicial review.** Judicial review is an important means of circumscribing irrational agency behavior.

### 2. Limitation on Judicial Review of Agency Discretion--Gilmore v. Lujan, 947 F.2d 1409 (9th Cir. 1991).

  a. **Facts.** Gilmore (P) applied for an oil and gas lease from the Bureau of Land Management ("BLM"). The BLM selected P's application at random and sent it to P to be manually signed and dated. The notice stated that P's offer would be rejected if the signed copies were not filed in the BLM's Reno office within 30 days. P signed the copies and sent them back by certified mail, with a return receipt requested. When P had not received the return receipt card by the morning of the deadline, his secretary called the BLM office and learned that the forms had not arrived. P could not travel to Reno by the end of the day. P's secretary claimed the BLM personnel said over the phone that they would accept a faxed signature, but the BLM personnel claimed they never said that. P faxed a signed form to a Reno attorney who physically gave it to the BLM. P sent signed originals by overnight mail, but the BLM rejected P's offer

Gilmore
v. Lujan

because the signed original was a day late. P appealed the decision, but the Interior Board of Land Appeals upheld the denial without deciding the facts of the disputed phone conversations because parties dealing with the government are chargeable with knowledge of applicable regulations. P sought judicial review by suing Lujan (D), Secretary of the Interior, in federal court. The district court affirmed, and P appeals.

    **b.**    **Issue.** May a court overturn an agency's decision that is within the agency's lawful discretion under its regulations?

    **c.**    **Held.** No. Judgment affirmed.

        1)    The BLM regulation specifically requires that all applications be holographically signed in ink by the potential lessee, and that machine signatures shall not be used. This provides fair notice to all applicants that failure to comply would result in denial of their applications.

        2)    P's application submitted over the fax machine was not holographic but created by a machine. D has discretion not to depart from the regulation.

        3)    Courts have a narrow scope of review of agency decisions. The equities favor P, since he was not negligent in using the United States mail. He mailed the originals from Nebraska to Nevada with eight days to spare, which should have been enough time. And there would be no harm to the BLM if it accepted P's fax. Still, the courts have no authority to overrule an agency decision that is within its lawful discretion.

    **d.**    **Comment.** This case illustrates the power administrative agencies can have over the lives of those they affect, and the relative impotence of the courts even to do equity. The court in this case stated that the "hands" of the BLM "are more iron than velvet." The court went on to say, "We can only suggest to [the] BLM that the body politic would not be put at risk by the granting of relief in these narrow and rare situations."

**3.**    **Focus on Procedure.** Administrative law focuses on procedure because it is concerned with keeping administrative agencies within the constraints established by Congress. Protecting individuals against agencies that exceed their authority requires understanding the procedures agencies must comply with. Agencies generate enormous amounts of detailed substantive law that can only be covered by in-depth examination of the particular field of substantive law. Focusing on how agencies create and enforce laws provides a critical background for understanding the substantive laws in any particular case, and what avenues of challenge are available.

## B. ADMINISTRATIVE AGENCIES

1. **Introduction.** Federal administrative agencies are defined by APA section 551 by what they are not; they do not consist of the legislature, the courts, or the governments of the states or the District of Columbia. The "headless fourth branch" of our federal government, administrative agencies employ more people, dispense more money, and regulate more activities than perhaps the other three combined.

   a. **Powers of agencies.** Many (but not all) agencies have been given both quasi-judicial and quasi-legislative authority. The former includes the power to decide controversies between parties. The latter involves the power to promulgate rules and regulations which, like statutes, have the force and effect of law.

   b. **Effect of agency rules.** Agency rules have the force and effect of law so long as they are constitutional, were promulgated in a procedurally proper manner, and do not stray beyond the authority conferred by the legislature (*i.e.*, they are not ultra vires).

2. **Appointment.** All officers of the United States must be appointed by the President with the advice and consent of the Senate. Congress may vest the appointment of interior officers in the President alone, the courts, or the heads of departments. [U.S. Const. Art. II, §2]

3. **Civil Service System.** In 1883, Congress established the Civil Service System so as to reduce abuses of the "spoils system" of political patronage appointments. Under the system, appointment is ostensibly determined by merit, and removal is severely circumscribed. Almost 85% of federal employees fall under its umbrella. Excessive job security has been criticized as breeding lethargy among low and midlevel government workers.

4. **Removal of Appointed Officers.**

   a. **General rule.** Most executive branch appointees may be freely removed by the President without cause. In *Myers v. United States*, 272 U.S. 52 (1926), the Supreme Court struck down a law conditioning removal of postmasters upon Senate approval thereof. The court held that this requirement was inconsistent with the "executive power" conferred to the President by the Constitution, and his duty to take care that the "laws are faithfully executed." The President has absolute power of removal over appointees in the higher echelon of the executive branch.

   b. **Limitation.** The President ordinarily may not remove appointees to the independent regulatory commissions without cause. In *Humphrey's Executor v. United States*, 295 U.S. 602 (1935), the

Supreme Court held unlawful President Franklin Roosevelt's removal of Humphrey from the Federal Trade Commission prior to the expiration of his seven-year term of office, for the statute conditioned removal on "inefficiency, neglect of duty, or malfeasance in office," of which there was none on the part of Commissioner Humphrey.

Freytag v.
Commissioner
of Internal
Revenue

5. **Appointment of Special Trial Judges--Freytag v. Commissioner of Internal Revenue,** 501 U.S. 868 (1991).

    a. **Facts.** Freytag and others (Ps) were assessed with federal income tax deficiencies by the Commissioner of Internal Revenue. They sought review in Tax Court and their cases were assigned to a Tax Court Judge. The Tax Court had been created by Congress and consists of 19 judges appointed to 15-year terms by the President, by and with the advice and consent of the Senate. The judge became ill, and the chief judge of the Tax Court assigned a Special Trial Judge to preside over the case, at first to take evidence and then to prepare written findings and an opinion. Congress had authorized the chief judge to appoint and assign these special trial judges, formerly known as commissioners. The special trial judge concluded that Ps' tax shelter scheme was a sham and that Ps owed taxes. The chief judge adopted the opinion as that of the Tax Court. The Fifth Circuit affirmed and the Supreme Court granted certiorari.

    b. **Issue.** May Congress grant the chief judge of the United States Tax Court authority to appoint special trial judges?

    c. **Held.** Yes. Judgment affirmed.

        1) Ps claim that if the statute allows a special trial judge to preside over Tax Court trials, then it violates the Appointments Clause of the Constitution, which requires the President to appoint Officers of the United States. The Clause allows inferior Officers to be appointed by the President, the Courts of Law, or the Heads of Departments.

        2) Because their office and duties are specified by statute, and because they exercise significant discretion as part of those duties, special trial judges are "inferior Officers" whose appointment must conform to the Appointments Clause.

        3) The Tax Court is not a department in the Executive Branch. The limitation in the Appointments Clause was intended to preserve accountability. If every agency or organ of the Executive Branch is deemed a "Department," the purpose of the Appointments Clause would be undermined. Instead, the term "Department" refers only to a Cabinet-level department.

4) Congress clearly intended to make the Tax Court an Article I legislative court. The Appointments Clause does not limit the term "Courts of Law" to those established under Article III. Non-Article III tribunals, such as the Court of Claims, exercise the judicial power of the United States. As an Article I court, the Tax Court also exercises the judicial power and is a Court of Law. Because it performs exclusively judicial functions, allowing the Tax Court to appoint "inferior Officers" does not undermine the constitutional limitation on the appointment power.

## C. TYPES OF AGENCIES

1. **Multi-Member vs. Single-Head Agencies.** Administrative agencies generally fall into two structural categories.

    a. **Single-head agencies.** Most administrative agencies of the executive branch, (*e.g.,* Departments of Labor and Agriculture) are headed by a single individual appointed by the President. These individuals may be removed from office without cause.

    b. **Multi-member commissions.** Most independent regulatory commissions (*e.g.,* ICC, SEC, FTC) are composed of several individuals (usually an odd number), no more than a simple majority of whom may be members of a single political party. Once appointed to their staggered, multi-year terms, they ordinarily may not be removed by the President without cause (*e.g.,* inefficiency, neglect of duty, or malfeasance in office).

2. **Regulatory vs. Nonregulatory Agencies.**

    a. **Regulatory agencies.** Regulatory agencies are usually vested with comprehensive jurisdiction to regulate a wide spectrum of economic activities of specific industries.

        1) **Interstate Commerce Commission.** The Interstate Commerce Commission ("ICC") was the first independent regulatory commission created by Congress. It was established in 1887.

        2) **The "big seven."** Since then, several major agencies have been established by Congress utilizing the ICC as a model. The Federal Trade Commission ("FTC") was created in 1914, and five major regulatory agencies were established during the administration of Franklin Roosevelt: Federal Power Commission ("FPC"), Federal Communications Commission ("FCC"), Securities and Exchange Commission ("SEC"), National Labor Relations Board ("NLRB"), and Civil Aeronautics Board ("CAB"). Collectively, the big seven regulate the major indus-

tries of the United States economy: communications, transportation, and energy. The responsibilities of the FPC were transferred to the nascent Federal Energy Regulatory Commission of the Department of Energy in 1977. The jurisdiction of the CAB was transferred to the United States Department of Transportation in 1985.

**3)** **State administrative agencies.** Each state usually has comparable intra-state jurisdiction vested in a single administrative agency, frequently named the state Public Utilities Commission. Many are modeled after the first such federal agency, the ICC.

**4)** **Regulatory powers.** Economic regulation can be divided into three categories.

    **a)** **Licensing.** Most regulatory agencies regulate entry into the affected industry by issuing certificates of "public convenience and necessity" to successful applicants.

    **b)** **Ratemaking.** Many such agencies establish both maximum and minimum rates to be charged the consumers of such products.

    **c)** **Business practices.** Many agencies have been given comprehensive jurisdiction over a multitude of corporate practices of the regulated industries, including purchases, mergers, consolidations, interlocking directorates, stock issuances, and various antitrust activities.

**5)** **Regulatory power widely held.** Although almost all independent regulatory agencies hold these powers, several executive branch agencies do as well (*e.g.*, Department of Agriculture).

**6)** **Social regulation.** More recent in origin than agencies conducting economic regulation are those agencies dedicated to the regulation of nonmarket behavior by business enterprises (*e.g.*, Environmental Protection Agency ("EPA"), Occupational Safety and Health Administration ("OSHA")). Health, environmental, and safety regulation attempts to force business to internalize the costs of public interest protection rather than perpetuating the "tragedy of the Commons."

**b.** **Nonregulatory agencies.** These agencies typically dispense money (*e.g.*, government insurance and pensions) to promote social and economic welfare. Benefactors to individuals fall into three categories.

**1)** Employee protection "workers' compensation" and other economic schemes designed to protect the individual from the hazards of employment.

**2)** Social insurance, Social Security, and unemployment compensation.

3) Welfare and veterans' assistance.

**3. Development of Administrative Law in the United States.** In the United States, administrative law has undergone three distinct periods of development.

   **a. Pre-1936.** The emphasis in administrative law was on constitutional questions of delegations of power.

   **b. Post-*Morgan (see infra)* cases.** For 40 years, the emphasis was on administrative procedure, particularly after the enactment of the Administrative Procedure Act ("APA") in 1946.

   **c. Contemporary era.** Deregulation and regulatory reform are perennial political movements. Social welfare, consumer, and environmental regulation has become more prominent than traditional economic regulation.

## D. AGENCIES AND INDEPENDENCE

**1. Basic Principles.** The Constitution establishes three distinct branches of government: the Legislative, the Judicial, and the Executive. Administrative agencies are to some extent a combination of these. Created by Congress, they administer the law in an executive capacity, they create the law by issuing regulations, and they interpret the law by means of administrative law judges ("ALJs"). Because agencies are not run by elected officials, some commentators deem them unaccountable to the public. In fact, their independence has made administrative agencies attractive targets of delegation of controversial decisionmaking responsibilities. The Supreme Court has been sensitive to the separation of powers problems, however.

**2. Attempted Delegation of Budget Decisionmaking--Bowsher v. Synar,** 478 U.S. 714 (1986). Bowsher v. Synar

   **a. Facts.** Congress enacted the Gramm-Rudman-Hollings Act, or Balanced Budget and Emergency Deficit Control Act of 1985, which was intended to eliminate the federal budget deficit. The Act established a maximum deficit amount for each fiscal year from 1986 through 1991. Should the deficit exceed the maximum in any year, across-the-board cuts in spending would automatically reduce the deficit to the targeted level. The reductions would be accomplished based on calculations made by the Office of Management and Budget ("OMB") and the Congressional Budget Office ("CBO"), which would be presented to the Comptroller General, who in turn would report to the President. The President would have to issue a sequestration order implementing the recommended spending reductions unless Congress otherwise reduced spending. Shortly after the President signed the Act, Congressman Synar (P) sought a declaratory judgment that the Act was unconstitutional. The district court held that the Comptroller General's role violated the separation of powers doctrine. The Supreme Court granted certiorari.

**b.** **Issue.** May Congress ~~cannot~~ delegate its power to appropriate public funds to an administrative agency?

**c.** **Held.** No. Judgment affirmed.

1) The constitutional separation of powers into three branches was intended to assure full and open debate on public issues as well as to provide checks and balances in the exercise of governmental power.

2) Congress was not intended to actively supervise executive officers. The Senate advises and consents with respect to presidential appointment of Officers of the United States, but it can remove them only upon impeachment and conviction. Any further congressional role is inconsistent with the separation of powers.

3) Due to the limited authority Congress has over executive officers, Congress may not vest the authority to execute the law in an officer who is answerable only to Congress. Otherwise, Congress would be able to execute its laws in violation of the Constitution. If an officer controlled by Congress could execute the laws, Congress would have a congressional veto, which was declared unconstitutional in *INS v. Chadha*, (*infra*).

4) The Comptroller General is nominated by the President and confirmed by the Senate, but he is removable only by Congress. The Comptroller General is an officer of Congress because Congress has the power of removal. For that reason, the Comptroller General may not be entrusted with executive powers.

5) Under the Act, the Comptroller General must prepare a report containing detailed estimates of the projected federal deficit as well as the reductions necessary to reduce the deficit to the target guidelines. He acts independently in evaluating the inputs from the OMB and the CBO. This function is executive; the Comptroller General interprets the law to implement the legislative mandate. In fact, the President is required to implement the Comptroller General's directive.

6) By retaining control in this manner over the execution of the Act, Congress has improperly intruded into the executive function.

_[handwritten margin notes:]_

Congress cannot reserve for itself ē power of removal of an officer charged w/ ē execution of ē laws except by impeachment (pp33)

Congress can administer agency:
1) reduce funding
2) Impeachment
3) Amend ē legislation
4) Oversight hearing ⇒ bring them in ½ ask question

Once they passed legislation for an agency to do executive work, Congress cannot retain removal authority

**3. Creation of Independent Counsel--Morrison v. Olson,** 487 U.S. 654 (1988).

Morrison v. Olson

a. **Facts.** The Ethics in Government Act of 1978, 28 U.S.C. sections 591 *et seq.*, provided for the appointment of an "independent counsel" to investigate and prosecute specified government officials for violations of federal criminal law. Under the Act, the Attorney General conducts a preliminary investigation of possible violations, and then reports to the Special Division, a court created by the Act. If the Attorney General determines that there are reasonable grounds to believe further investigation or a prosecution is warranted, then he applies for appointment of independent counsel. The Special Division then appoints such counsel and defines the counsel's prosecutorial jurisdiction. The independent prosecutor is required to comply with Department of Justice policies to the extent possible. The Attorney General may remove an independent prosecutor for cause; otherwise, the counsel's tenure expires upon completion of the specified investigations or prosecutions. The counsel notifies the Attorney General of the completion; alternatively, the Special Division may find the task completed. Certain congressional committees have oversight jurisdiction regarding the independent counsel's conduct. Pursuant to this Act, the Special Division appointed Morrison (D) to investigate allegations that Olson (P), an assistant attorney general, had lied in testimony to Congress. D obtained a grand jury subpoena against P. P moved to quash the subpoenas, claiming that D had no authority to proceed because the Act was unconstitutional. The trial court upheld the Act, but the court of appeals reversed. D appeals.

b. **Issue.** May Congress may provide for the judicial appointment of independent counsel for purposes of investigating and prosecuting federal criminal offenses?

c. **Held.** Yes. Judgment reversed.

1) Under the Appointments Clause, there are two classes of officers: (i) principal officers, who are selected by the President with the advice and consent of the Senate; and (ii) inferior officers whom Congress may allow to be appointed by the President alone, by the heads of departments, or by the Judiciary. Thus, if D is a principal officer, the Act violates the Constitution.

2) The difference between principal and inferior officers is not always clear. It requires consideration of several factors:

   a) D may be removed by a higher Executive Branch official, despite having independent powers.

    b)    D's authority is limited to performing specified, limited duties. D has no policymaking authority and must comply to Department of Justice policies.

    c)    D's office is limited in jurisdiction to the terms of the appointment. It is also limited in tenure; it does not extend beyond the completion of the specific task given.

    d)    Evaluation of these factors leads to the conclusion that an independent counsel is an inferior officer. However, P claims that Congress may not provide that an officer of one branch be appointed by officers of another branch.

3)    The Clause itself does not forbid interbranch appointments, but instead gives Congress discretion to determine the propriety of vesting the appointment of executive officials in the courts. The limitation on this power is where it implicates the separation of powers or impairs the constitutional functions assigned to one of the branches. The very reason for the Act was to remove the appointment power from the executive branch, and the judicial branch is the most logical alternative. By making members of the Special Division ineligible to participate in any matters relating to an independent counsel they have appointed, Congress has protected the separation of powers.

4)    Article III limits the judicial power to cases and controversies. However, if the appointments clause gives Congress the power to authorize the courts to appoint officials such as an independent counsel, which it does, the appointment power is a source of authority independent of Article III. The additional powers granted to the Special Division, such as defining the counsel's authority and tenure of office, are incidental to the exercise of the appointment power itself.

5)    The Special Division also has power to terminate an independent counsel's office, which is an administrative power. This power must be narrowly construed to avoid constitutional problems. It is thus limited to removing an independent counsel who has served her purpose, but does not acknowledge that fact and remains on the payroll.

6)    P also asserts a separation of powers problem because the Attorney General can remove an independent counsel only by showing "good cause." In *Bowsher* (*supra*), for example, Congress could not involve itself in the removal of an executive officer. Under the Act in this case, however, Congress did not acquire a removal power over executive officials beyond its power of impeachment and conviction.

7)    The Attorney General retains the removal power, subject to the good cause requirement. But the Constitution does not give the President unbridled discretion to remove officials of independent agencies. Prior cases have distinguished purely executive officials from quasi-legislative and quasi-judicial

officials, but this is an inappropriate distinction for analyzing removal powers. The proper question is whether the removal restrictions impede the President's ability to perform his constitutional duty. Because the independent counsel has a limited function, and because the Attorney General has removal authority for good cause, the good cause restriction does not unconstitutionally impede the President.

8) The second separation of powers issue is based on interference with the role of the executive branch. However, the Act does not permit either congressional or judicial usurpation of executive functions. It also leaves the executive branch with the ability to supervise the counsel's prosecutorial powers.

## 4. Enforcement Authority--FTC v. American National Cellular, Inc., 810 F.2d 1511 (9th Cir. 1987).

a. **Facts.** The FTC (P) filed suit for preliminary and permanent injunctions against American National Cellular, Inc. (D). P claimed that D violated section 5(a) of the Federal Trade Commission Act because it persuaded investors to use D's services in an FCC license lottery without disclosing the high risk nature of the investment. P claimed that D intentionally misled investors. D answered that the Act permitting P to bring suit violated the Constitution because enforcement is reserved to the executive branch, of which P is not a part. The district court upheld P's enforcement authority. D appeals.

b. **Issue.** May an administrative agency *may* exercise enforcement authority granted by Congress?

c. **Held.** Yes. Judgment affirmed.

1) D claims that when P sought injunctive relief for an alleged violation of federal law, P was enforcing that law contrary to the separation of powers, which permits only the executive to enforce the law.

2) In *Humphrey's Executor v. United States*, 295 U.S. 602 (1935), President Roosevelt had tried to remove Humphrey as FTC Commissioner. The Court ultimately held that when Congress established the FTC, it created an agency free of executive authority except in its selection. Congress limited the President's power to remove agency heads, but did not limit his appointment power. The FTC was held constitutional. This ruling has been followed ever since.

*[handwritten left margin: limit President's power to remove for cause!]*

*[handwritten right margin: Congress intended a body which shall be independent of executive authority, except in its selection, & free to exercise its judgmt w/ leave/hinderance of any other official /dept of ê gov]*

3) In *Bowsher* (*supra*), the Court held that because Congress had reserved to itself the power of removal of the officer charged with execution of the laws, the scheme violated the separation of powers doctrine. Contrary to the scheme in that case, the FTC Commis-

officers of ē US, inc FTC commissioners, who are appointed by ē President w/ advice ? consent of ē Senate, ? are subj to congressional removal only by impeachment, may engage in enforcement of fed. law.

sioners are removable by Congress only through the impeachment process. Accordingly, the FTC may properly enforce the law.

**5.  Characteristics of Administrative Agencies.**

    **a.  Size.** Most federal administrative agencies have several hundred to several thousand employees.

    **b.  Specialization.** Typically, an agency focuses on a particular industry or specialized problems, and is expected to develop expertise therein.

    **c.  Responsibility for results.** Congress usually identifies objectives it expects the administrative agency to satisfy.

    **d.  Variety of duties.** Agencies frequently engage in adjudication, rulemaking, and the performance of quasi-executive administrative functions.

    **e.  Heavy workload.** Most agencies have a congested docket composed of scores of proceedings, some of which may be of considerable complexity.

Administrative agency's stages of existence (pp 49)

① Born
    ↓

Adolescence : complacency + tiredness
    ↓

maturity : processes become institutionally ratinized + conformity to bureaucratic norms.
    ↓

die (Hardly ever die)

# II. DELEGATION OF POWERS

## A. INTRODUCTION

Administrative agency jurisdiction is limited by the scope of the statutes that confer agency authority. The statutes both establish and limit agency authority. If the agency strays beyond the authority so conferred, it acts ultra vires and therefore, unlawfully.

## B. LEGISLATIVE POWER

Although many courts have suggested that lawmaking authority is exclusively a function of the legislature, significant powers of lawmaking have been delegated to administrative agencies. Most federal agencies hold power to promulgate rules and regulations that have the force and effect of law.

**1. Separation and Delegation.**

   **a. Separation of powers.** The constitutional doctrine of separation of powers insists that governmental power be divided among the three branches of government: the executive, legislative, and judicial. Although the doctrine, strictly construed, would seem to prohibit delegation of quasi-legislative or quasi-judicial authority of administrative agencies, in practice such authority is widely delegated.

   **b. Unlawful delegation.** Delegation has been held to be unconstitutionally broad on occasion, particularly when the legislature fails to identify precise standards to govern the exercise thereof.

   **c. Oil transportation--Panama Refining Co. v. Ryan,** 293 U.S. 388 (1935).

      **1) Facts.** Panama Refining Co. (P), a Texas oil refiner, sued Ryan and other federal officials (Ds) to enjoin enforcement of regulations promulgated by the Secretary of the Interior pursuant to section 9(c) of the National Industrial Recovery Act ("NIRA"). The section enabled the President to prohibit the transportation of petroleum and petroleum products in an amount exceeding that authorized to be produced by any state. Violation resulted in fine and/or imprisonment. P argued that the NIRA constituted an unconstitutional delegation of legislative power to the President.

      **2) Issue.** May Congress ~~grant~~ cannot the President authority to take action without establishing standards to govern that action?

      **3) Held.** No.

a)   Congress neither established standards to govern the President's action, nor was the President obligated to make specific findings prior to acting. No conditions precedent to the President's action were specified. Therefore, the states were left with the determination of whether production should be permitted.

b)   Under the NIRA the President held unlimited authority to implement the prohibition, and disobedience of his determination would be punishable by fine or imprisonment. The absence of standards governing his exercise of power, if upheld, could allow the legislature to delegate power to regulate virtually any commercial activity to the President.

4)   **Dissent** (Cardozo, J.). The legislation must specify reasonably clear standards to govern the President's discretion. Such standards are found in the NIRA. The President's means of implementing the statute's specific policies were limited to prohibiting the transportation of specified commodities, and only then if the affected state had limited production thereof. The policy of Congress, express or implied, is sufficient to make the delegation valid.

2.   **Contingent Delegation.** Frequently, delegation of legislative power is limited by stated factual contingencies or conditions. So long as the precise contingency is identified by the enabling legislation, courts have generally been willing to uphold the delegation.

3.   **Subordinate Delegation.** Many agencies have been granted quasi-legislative authority to promulgate rules and regulations to implement the legislative scheme. These have been generally upheld by the courts, in part because of the pragmatic recognition that Congress is unable to provide the plethora of details required for the proper administration of government.

4.   **Excessive Delegation.**

a.   **General rule.** A delegation of legislative authority that is found to be wholly without standards specifying conditions pursuant to which it is to be exercised is unconstitutional.

Schechter Poultry Corp. v. United States

b.   **Unlimited authority--Schechter Poultry Corp. v. United States,** 295 U.S. 495 (1935).

1)   **Facts.** Schechter Poultry Corp. (D) was convicted of violating the "Live Poultry Code" promulgated under the NIRA. The NIRA delegated to the President authority to approve "codes of fair competition" upon application by a trade or industrial group, provided that (i) the group imposes no inequitable restriction on membership, and (ii) the code is not designed to promote monopolies or suppress competition, and will serve to effectuate the policies of NIRA.

2) **Issue.** May Congress delegate power to the President to take action without providing adequate definitions of the subjects to which the exercise of authority is to be addressed?

3) **Held.** No.

    a) There are no limitations on the things that could be subject to "Codes of Fair Competition," nor are there statutory standards identifying the conduct the codes were to prescribe.

    b) Moreover, no procedural safeguards were identified for promulgation of the codes. This is unlike similar authority held by the FTC, for that agency offers procedural protection to the parties before it.

4) **Concurrence** (Cardozo, J.). The delegation here, in contrast to that in Panama, is "unconfined and vagrant" and "delegation run riot." Here, the authority delegated was not confined to any specified acts or standards. The legislature seemed to create a "roving commission to inquire into evils and upon discovery correct them."

5. **Post-1935 Federal Cases.** Only in *Panama* and *Schechter Poultry* has the United States Supreme Court concluded that delegations have been unconstitutional. Nevertheless, the delegation doctrine has never been overruled. Moreover, *Schechter Poultry* addressed perhaps the most liberal delegation in United States history. Hence, it marks a line beyond which the legislature may not go in delegating authority. However, many post-1935 cases on the issue of delegation appear to embrace the philosophy expressed by Justice Cardozo in his dissent in *Panama*.

    a. **Statement of purpose.** *Yakus v. United States*, 321 U.S. 414 (1944), upheld the constitutionality of the Emergency Price Control Act of 1942 ("EPC"). Under the EPC, the Price Administrator was granted jurisdiction to establish maximum prices on commodities when the prices rose or threatened to rise to a level inconsistent with the purpose of the Act. EPC section 1 provided that its purposes were to stabilize prices, prohibit their abnormal increase, eliminate profiteering, and so on. Chief Justice Stone, writing for the Supreme Court, concluded that the standards expressed in the EPC coupled with the statement of considerations required to be made by the Administrator were "sufficiently definite and precise to enable Congress, the courts and the public to ascertain whether the Administrator, in fixing the designated prices, had conformed to those standards. . . ." Accordingly, the statute was upheld as a lawful delegation. Justice Roberts filed a vigorous dissent in which he argued that the EPC "set no limits upon the discretion or judgment of the Administrator."

**b.** **Flexibility necessary.** In *Lichter v. United States*, 334 U.S. 742 (1948), the Supreme Court upheld the constitutionality of the Renegotiation Act of 1942, which delegated to administrative officers the power to recover "excessive profits" on the renegotiation of war contracts. The Court held that it was not necessary that the legislature "supply administrative officials with a specific formula for their guidance in a field where flexibility and the adoption of the congressional policy to infinitely variable conditions constitute the essence of the program. . . ."

**c.** **Wartime delegations.** Both *Yakus* and *Lichter* were wartime delegations.

**d.** **Foreign affairs.** Decisions of the United States Supreme Court have suggested that the traditional limitations on congressional delegation may not apply in the area of foreign affairs.

Mistretta v. United States

3 functions :
if met proper delegation

**e.** **Delegation to independent commission--Mistretta v. United States,** 488 U.S. 361 (1989).

**1)** **Facts.** Mistretta (D) was convicted of federal offenses related to a cocaine sale. He challenged the constitutionality of the Sentencing Reform Act of 1984. The Act changed federal sentencing procedures by imposing determinate sentences established by the United States Sentencing Commission, which are binding on the courts unless the judge in a given case provides specific reasons for imposing a sentence different from that described in the guideline. The Act also limited appellate review of the sentence by allowing defendants to appeal only sentences that are above the defined range, and by allowing the Government to appeal a sentence that is below the range. The Commission is an independent commission in the judicial branch whose members are appointed by the President by and with the advice and consent of the Senate. Three of the members are federal judges selected from a list of six judges recommended to the President by the Judicial Conference. The district court denied D relief. The Supreme Court granted certiorari.

**2)** **Issue.** May Congress ~~may~~ delegate to an independent commission the authority to establish determinate sentences for federal crimes?

**3)** **Held.** Yes. Judgment affirmed.

    a) The nondelegation doctrine reflects the principle of separation of powers and prevents Congress from delegating its legislative power to another branch of government. It does not prevent Congress from obtaining the assistance of its coordinate branches, however, so long as Congress establishes an "intelligible principle" to which the entity receiving the delegated authority is required to conform.

b) Applications of the "intelligible principle" test are guided by the reality that in a complex society, Congress cannot do its job without being able to delegate power under broad general directives. With the exception of two statutes invalidated in 1935, the Court has always upheld Congress' ability to delegate power under broad standards.

c) In this Act, Congress gave the Commission three goals to be attained by sentencing, as well as four specific purposes of sentencing: to reflect the seriousness of the offense, to promote respect of the law, and to provide just punishment for the offense; to afford adequate deterrence to criminal conduct; to protect the public from further crimes of the defendant; and to provide the defendant with needed correctional treatment.

d) Congress also prescribed the specific tool for the Commission to use in regulating sentencing by establishing the guidelines system. The Commission was specifically directed to develop sentencing ranges for each category of offense involving each category of defendant, and imposed a constraint such that the maximum sentence shall not exceed the minimum by more that 25% or six months (except that a life sentence is permissible if the minimum term is 30 years or more). Congress went further and required the Commission to consider seven factors in formulating offense categories, and included specific guidelines for certain offenses and criminals, such as repeat offenders.

e) While the Commission may have significant discretion in formulating guidelines, Congress has set forth more than merely an "intelligible principle." The Act explains what the Commission should do, how it should do it, and sets forth specific directives to govern particular situations. It is appropriate for Congress to delegate the complicated task of developing proportionate penalties for hundreds of different crimes by a variety of criminals. The involvement of the judicial branch does not violate the system of checks and balances.

4) **Dissent** (Scalia, J.). Under the Constitution, basic policy decisions governing society are to be made by Congress. While some judgments involving policy considerations must be left to the officers executing the law and to the judges applying it, delegation becomes unconstitutional once it exceeds the limit required by the inherent necessities of governmental coordination and common sense. Clearly, the Constitution does not allow any branch other than Congress to make laws. There is no acceptable delegation of legislative power, but the Act is a pure delegation of legislative power. The Commission does not exercise judicial or executive powers; it just makes the laws regarding sentencing. If the delegation of such rulemaking is upheld, Congress will be encouraged to create other "expert" bodies, a kind of junior-varsity Congress, that are also insulated from the political process and give them the authority to create laws in areas that are politically difficult.

**6. Federal Delegation: A Caveat.**

a. **Judicial deference to Congress.** No federal court has struck down the doctrine, and most express a need for the legislature to fulfill its requirements. Even when a statute is apparently standardless, a court may uphold the statute by finding standards.

b. **Vocal minority.** Although the Supreme Court has not struck down a federal statute as an unconstitutional delegation since *Panama* and *Schechter Poultry*, its application has been advocated by some Justices.

c. **Agencies cannot determine basic policy issues--Industrial Department v. American Petroleum Institute,** 448 U.S. 607 (1980).

1) **Facts.** The American Petroleum Institute (P) brought a pre-enforcement challenge to a safety standard promulgated by the Secretary of Labor under the Occupational Safety and Health Act. The Act provides that the Secretary "shall set the standard which most adequately assures to the extent feasible . . . that no employee will suffer material impairment of health." The Secretary interpreted this to impose a duty to set the standard for permissible exposure to substances such as benzene for which no safe level is known at the lowest level that can be achieved at bearable cost with available technology. P claimed that the Act requires the Secretary to demonstrate that any particular health standard is justifiable on the basis of a rough balancing of costs and benefits. The court of appeals held the standard invalid. The Supreme Court granted certiorari.

2) **Issue.** May Congress cannot delegate the authority to regulate worker exposure to chemicals and leave it up to the delegatee to determine basic policy issues?

3) **Held.** No. Judgment affirmed.

a) John Locke argued that the legislature's power is to make laws, not legislators, and this principal has been accepted by the Court. However, the Court has permitted Congress to delegate authority to the executive branch where the field involved is so technical that it is impractical for Congress to do anything more than establish the general policy and standards behind the law and let the agency refine and apply the standards to particular cases.

b) In this case, however, Congress has simply asked the Secretary to adopt the most protective standard if he can, but if he cannot, he is excused. Where no "safe" level is known, Congress provides no guidance. The legislative history does not provide any guidance, and there are no other statutory contexts, other than a vague preference for safety over costs.

c) The nondelegation doctrine serves the important functions of ensuring that important choices of social policy be made by Congress, the branch of Government most responsive to the popular will. It also guarantees that the recipient of delegated authority from Congress will receive an "intelligible principle" to guide the exercise of the delegated discretion, and gives the courts something against which to review the exercise of delegated authority. The legislation in this case fails to fulfill any of these important functions.

**4) Comment.** Although no other Justices joined Justice Rehnquist's opinion, it was the fifth opinion in a plurality that invalidated the standard. Four Justices dissented. The other plurality opinions invalidated the standard because it was not supported by appropriate findings and lacked a cost-benefit analysis.

**d. Narrowing.** Some courts have held the authority delegated to be circumscribed so as to avoid these constitutional questions; for example, in *Kent v. Dulles*, 357 U.S. 116 (1958), the Supreme Court restrictively interpreted the Passport Act of 1926 as not allowing the promulgation of regulations by the Secretary of State limiting the travel opportunities of Communists.

**e. Unconstitutional delegation--American Trucking Association v. EPA,** 175 F.3d 1027 (D.C. Cir. 1999).

American Trucking Association v. EPA

**1) Facts.** The Environmental Protection Agency ("EPA") issued rules revising the primary and secondary national ambient air quality standards ("NAAQS") for particulate matter ("PM") and ozone. The statute required the EPA to establish the NAAQS at the level "requisite to protect the public health" with an "adequate margin of safety."

**2) Issue.** Has the EPA articulated an "intelligible principle" to guide its application of these criteria, or is one apparent from the statute?

**3) Held.** No. Hence, this is an unconstitutional delegation of legislative power. Case remanded.

a) The only concentration for PM and ozone that is totally risk free is zero. For the EPA to adopt any standard other than zero requires an explanation of the degree of imperfection permitted, which the EPA has failed to provide.

b) The EPA should adopt intelligible principles to guide its exercise of discretion. It may not adopt a cost-benefit analysis, but it may choose to eradicate any hint of direct health risk. However, a "one size fits all" criterion would not be desirable. The EPA should be able to adopt the equivalent of a generic unit of harm that evaluates the population affected, with the severity and probability of harm.

    **4) Dissent.** This statute and the EPA's establishment of NAAQS has been passed on by this court on numerous occasions, and never heretofore found to be an unconstitutional. The delegation doctrine has not been used to achieve this result in 64 years.

**7. State Delegation.** Most state courts have been more aggressive than federal courts in reversing delegations where standards to govern the exercise of authority have been vague, although some state courts have followed the more permissive modern federal approach.

State v.
Broom

    **a. Definition of crimes not delegable--State v. Broom,** 439 So. 2d 357 (La. 1983).

        **1) Facts.** State law regulated explosives and provided that the director of public safety would establish specific regulations that are "reasonably necessary" to protect the public's health, welfare, and safety. A state regulation promulgated under authority of this law prohibited operators of conveyances transporting explosives from leaving the vehicle unattended. Violations were punishable by fine or imprisonment or both. Broom (D), was charged with violating this regulation, which constituted a felony, by leaving his vehicle to get some food at a restaurant. The trial court dismissed the charges and the State (P) appeals.

        **2) Issue.** May the legislature delegate to an administrative official the authority to define felonies?

        **3) Held.** No. Judgment affirmed.

           a) The federal government has rejected the concept that delegation of legislative powers requires meaningful standards, but the state of Louisiana has not. The legislature cannot delegate to administrative bodies the right to define felony offenses.

           b) The law in this case unconstitutionally delegated authority to the director to define felony offenses. The law itself did not define the offense D was charged with; it simply provided grave penalties for undefined felonies. The exercise of governmental power must comply with the strict restraints established by the state constitution.

**8. Delegation and Standards.** Modern courts uphold virtually all delegations of legislative authority, except perhaps in areas affecting individual liberty or separation of powers. Nevertheless, the delegation doctrine remains as a reminder that in a representative form of government, standards of conduct should be prescribed by elected representatives instead of administrative agencies. Thus, it remains as a check against excessive delegation to administrative agencies.

## C. JUDICIAL POWER

Although there was once a vigorous debate over the issue of whether the legislature could delegate to an administrative agency anything but legislative power, the practice of delegating judicial power has since become widespread. The delegation of quasi-judicial power to administrative agencies has generally been upheld despite separation of powers objections.

1. **Binding Arbitration--Thomas v. Union Carbide Agricultural Products Co.,** 473 U.S. 568 (1985).

   Thomas v. Union Carbide Agricultural Products Co.

   a. **Facts.** When the EPA uses data submitted by private chemical companies for registration of pesticides, the Federal Insecticide, Fungicide and Rodenticide Act ("FIFRA") requires binding arbitration of the fees to be paid for the use of the data. Union Carbide Agricultural Products Co. and other chemical firms (Ps) submitted data to the EPA to obtain registration of pesticides. Ps were challenging the constitutionality of the statute that authorized data-sharing and public disclosure, and then amended their complaint to challenge the binding arbitration provisions. Ps claimed that Congress unconstitutionally gave judicial powers to arbitrators. The district court held the statute unconstitutional. D appeals.

   b. **Issue.** May Congress require binding arbitration between administrative agencies and private companies?

   c. **Held.** Yes. Judgment reversed.

      1) The Constitution does not require every federal question arising under federal law to be tried in an Article III court. Congress may vest decisionmaking authority in administrative tribunals.

      2) Ps claim that FIFRA gives them a private right to compensation that requires at least review by an Article III court. Under *Northern Pipeline Construction Co. v. Marathon Pipe Line Co.*, 458 U.S. 50 (1982), Ps claim that the only recognized exceptions to Article III adjudication are (i) military tribunals, (ii) territorial courts, and (iii) decisions involving public, not private, rights. This public rights/private rights test has never been adopted by a majority of the Court, however.

      3) Congressional delegation must be evaluated based on substance, not form. Congress may use a quasi-judicial method to resolve

matters that could be conclusively determined by the executive and legislative branches. P's right to compensation is not a traditional common law cause of action. Instead, it is an interest that is so closely integrated into the public regulatory scheme that it is a matter appropriate for agency resolution with limited involvement by Article III courts. Thus, the arbitration of Ps' right to compensation is not unconstitutional.

Granfinanciera
S.A. v. Nordberg

**2.    Right to Jury Trial--Granfinanciera S.A. v. Nordberg,** 492 U.S. 33 (1989).

    **a.    Facts.** Nordberg (P) became a trustee in bankruptcy. P sued Granfinanciera S.A. (D) and others for fraudulent conveyances, alleging that D had received $1.7 million from the debtor within one year of the date its bankruptcy petition was filed, without receiving consideration or reasonably equivalent value in return. The district court referred the proceedings to the bankruptcy court. D requested a trial by jury, but the bankruptcy judge denied the request on the ground that a suit to recover a fraudulent transfer is a core action that was originally a non-jury issue. The court entered judgment against D for $1.5 million. The district court and the court of appeals affirmed. The Supreme Court granted certiorari.

    **b.    Issue.** Does a defendant in a suit to recover a fraudulent conveyance from a bankrupt entity have a right to a jury trial when Congress has allowed a non-Article III tribunal to adjudicate such claims?

    **c.    Held.** Yes. Judgment reversed.

        1)    The Seventh Amendment preserves the right to a jury trial in all "suits at common law." This phrase means suits in which legal rights are ascertained as opposed to suits involving equitable rights alone. The analysis consists of comparing the statutory action to 18th century actions brought in the courts of England prior to the merger of law and equity, and then examining the remedy sought to determine whether it is legal or equitable in nature. If those two factors show that a party is entitled to a jury trial, the courts then decide whether Congress may assign, and has assigned, resolution of the relevant claim to a non-Article III adjudicative body that does not use a jury as a fact finder.

        2)    P's fraudulent conveyance suit seeks relief traditionally provided by the law courts, so the first part of the analysis suggests P should have a jury trial. However, Congress assigned adjudication to the Bankruptcy Court.

        3)    When Congress creates new statutory "public rights," it may assign their adjudication to a non-jury administrative agency. This power is limited to cases where "public rights" are litigated, meaning cases

in which the government is involved in its sovereign capacity under an otherwise valid statute creating enforceable public rights. Congress still cannot deny jury trials to parties who contest matters of private right.

4) The result of this analysis is the same as the analysis of whether Article III allows Congress to assign adjudication of the particular cause of action to a non-Article III tribunal. If a statutory cause of action is not a "public right" for Article III purposes, then Congress may not assign its adjudication to a specialized non-Article III court.

5) A case may involve "public rights" even if the federal government is not a party. Congress may create a seemingly "private" right that is so closely integrated into a public regulatory scheme as to be a matter appropriate for agency resolution with limited involvement by the Article III judiciary. But if the statutory right is not closely intertwined with a federal regulatory program and the right neither belongs to nor exists against the federal government, then it must be adjudicated by an Article III court. And if it is a legal right, the parties are guaranteed a jury trial.

6) The fraudulent conveyance suit is more a private than a public right, so D is entitled to a jury trial.

d. **Concurrence** (Scalia, J.). A "public right" can arise only between the government and others.

3. **Administrative Adjudication Is Not Judicial Function--McHugh v. Santa Monica Rent Control Board,** 777 P.2d 91 (Cal. 1989).

McHugh v. Santa Monica Rent Control Board

see pg 121

reject private right argument

a. **Facts.** McHugh (P), a landlord, received administrative complaints by two of his tenants. P appealed a hearing officer's orders to the Santa Monica Rent Control Board (D). D found that P had charged excess rents. P petitioned for a writ of mandate to compel D to set aside its decision and to enjoin D from acting on any complaints for excess rent. The trial court granted P's motion. D appeals.

b. **Issue.** May a city create an administrative board to adjudicate claims of excessive rent under a rent control statute?

c. **Held.** Yes. Judgment reversed.

1) The California Constitution vests the judicial power in the courts, and agencies not vested by the Constitution with judicial powers may not exercise such powers. The question is whether D exercised judicial powers.

*reasonable necessity / legit
regulatory purpose test:*

*- Whether ā challenged remedial
power is authorized by
legislation ξ*

*reasonably necessary to
accomplish ē agency's
regulatory purposes*

(2) Cases from other jurisdictions hold that an administrative agency does not exercise judicial powers when it makes restitutive money awards so long as making the awards is reasonably necessary to effectuate the agency's primary, legitimate regulatory purposes and the "essential" judicial power remains ultimately in the courts through review of agency determinations. This is a reasoned and workable test to measure challenges to administrative agencies under the judicial powers clause of the California Constitution.

(3) The courts have adopted a tolerant approach to the delegation of judicial powers in recognition of the need to accommodate administrative adjudication of certain disputes to alleviate demands on the traditional judicial system. While administrative agencies exercise "judicial-like" powers, and broad administrative powers are necessary in an increasingly complex government, agencies may exercise only those powers that are reasonably necessary to effectuate the agency's primary, legitimate regulatory purposes. This "substantive limitation" precludes a proliferation of agencies created to adjudicate specialized private disputes.

4) In this case, D heard complaints that P charged excess rents and determined that P in fact had done so. These actions were reasonably necessary to accomplish D's primary, legitimate regulatory purposes of setting and regulating minimum rents in the local housing market. D does not adjudicate other types of disputes, so it has not violated the limiting principles.

5) P claims that administrative adjudication of monetary relief claims violates the right to jury trial. However, if the exercise of administrative power meets the "substantive limitation" requirement, then the constitutional right to a jury trial does not preclude administrative adjudication. Even applying the federal "private vs. public" approach, the interests in rent control are "public" rights.

4. **Constraint on Agency Abuse.** Professors Carrow and Reese acknowledge that tremendous powers of the legislature, executive, and judiciary have been conferred upon the "headless fourth branch" of government, including the adjudication of valuable interests and the imposition of sanctions. Nevertheless, the other branches retain certain checks on aberrant administrative agencies.

a. **Legislature.** The legislature may amend or revoke the agency's enabling legislation.

b. **Judiciary.** The judiciary may ordinarily modify, reverse, or remand the agency's initial determination if it does not comply with the enabling legislation.

5. **Adjudication of Traffic Infractions--Rosenthal v. Hartnett,** 326 N.E.2d 811 (N.Y. 1975).

   a. **Facts.** Rosenthal (D) was found guilty of speeding by a hearing officer of the Department of Motor Vehicles (P) and was fined $15. By statute, the New York Legislature had authorized administrative adjudication of such violations. The statute also provided that the standard of proof at the hearing would be the "clear and convincing" test. The hearing officer's decision was affirmed on administrative review. D challenged the determination on grounds that he was denied due process. The trial court held the delegation of the judicial power unconstitutional. P appeals.

   b. **Issue.** May the legislature authorize administrative adjudication in lieu of judicial adjudication of traffic offense and establish the "clear and convincing evidence" test as the standard of guilt?

   c. **Held.** Yes. Judgment reversed.

   1) The legislature has concluded that the dockets of both traffic and criminal courts are congested. The administrative agency model is a more efficient and economical means of disposing of this type of case.

   2) Since substitution of an administrative agency for the courts is upheld as constitutional, the agency may employ administrative procedure rather than criminal procedure.

## D. REMEDIES AND PENALTIES

1. **Introduction.** Statutes normally contain some enforcement provision, such as specifying that a violation of the statute is punishable by a certain penalty. A statute that delegated legislative power normally will specify a penalty for violation of the statute or of a rule or regulation promulgated pursuant to the statute. The theory is that a violation of the rule or regulation is not a crime defined by an administrative officer but a violation of the statute itself. Under the United States Constitution, this theory has been upheld. [*See* United States v. Grimaud, 220 U.S. 506 (1911)] Not all of the states agree, however.

2. **Remedies.** Administrative agencies are not normally empowered to provide all the remedies that a court of law may provide. Although early courts held that the power to award damages may not be delegated to an administrative agency [*see* State v. Public Service Commission, 259 S.W. 445 (Mo. 1924)], a number of contemporary courts have upheld such delegation. However, even if the agency does award money damages to an aggrieved party, only the courts can execute the judgment.

**a.** **Agency adjudication without jury trial--Vainio v. Brookshire,** 852 P.2d 596 (Mont. 1993).

    **1)** **Facts.** Brookshire (P) worked for a lounge and casino owned by Helena Vainio, represented by her personal representative Vainio (D). P claimed she was sexually harassed by an employee of the casino and filed a complaint with the Human Rights Commission ("HRC"). The HRC held a hearing and made findings in P's favor. The HRC found Helena personally liable for the harassment and awarded P $20,000. D appealed the findings to the district court. The district court affirmed the HRC, and D appeals.

    **2)** **Issue.** May a legislature assign adjudication of statutory rights to administrative agencies, including the authority to impose money damages?

    **3)** **Held.** Yes. Judgment affirmed.

        **a)** P's claim was based on the Montana Human Rights Act, which does not grant a right to trial by jury for violations. Although a statutory right to a jury trial has subsequently been adopted, it did not apply to the incidents P claimed.

        **b)** The HRC has statutory authority to award "reasonable" damages within its discretion. Parties before the HRC have the right to judicial review of all final HRC orders. Thus, the HRC does not have unbridled authority to award damages and the delegation of this authority to the HRC is not an unlawful delegation of judicial and legislative powers.

        **c)** The Act provides that the HRC may issue orders to "require any reasonable measure to correct the discriminatory practice and to rectify any harm, pecuniary or otherwise, to the person discriminated against." This includes emotional distress damages, and the HRC's award was not clearly erroneous.

    **4)** **Concurrence and dissent.** The damages awarded in this case are the traditional form of relief offered in courts of law, and the Montana and United States Constitutions guarantee the right to a jury trial in such cases. Fundamental constitutional rights cannot be evaded simply by delegating the initial determination of damages to a state agency other than a district court. D was denied the constitutional right to have a jury trial on the issue of compensatory damages.

**b.** **Injunctions--In re Investigation of Lauricella,** 546 So. 2d 207 (La. Ct. App. 1989).

    **1)** **Facts.** Walsdorf (P), a police sergeant, claimed to the Civil Service Commission that her employer, the East Jefferson Levell District ("the District") discriminated against her on the basis of her sex when it selected a candidate for a supervisory position. She filed a second action claiming that Lauricella (D), the President of the District's Board of Commissioners, retaliated against P for her initial claim. The Commission ordered the District to cease retaliating against P. P later filed a third appeal with the Commission, based on specific harassment by D. The Commission found D in contempt of its order to cease retaliating against P and fined him $500. D appeals from the order.

2) **Issue.** If the state constitution that created the civil service commission does not specifically so provide, may such a commission impose a fine on a person who is not a classified civil service employee who is found to be in contempt of an order issued by the commission?

3) **Held.** No. Judgment reversed.

   a) The Civil Service Commission has adopted rules that allow it to punish contempt with economic penalties. Contempt is defined as the failure of "any person" to comply with a Commission order.

   b) The Commission was established by the Louisiana Constitution, which gives the Commission broad powers, including the power to impose penalties for violation of its rules. However, the penalty power is limited to removal, suspension, and demotion, with loss of pay.

   c) Administrative agencies generally do not have power to impose punishment for contempt, unless expressly granted. The Louisiana Constitution does not grant the Commission the power and authority of courts, except as specifically granted, and it certainly does not grant the power to punish for contempt. The Commission can ensure compliance with its orders only through a court order or a criminal prosecution.

4) **Comment.** Some state courts have refused to allow delegation of the power to impose fines or penalties where the agency is given a discretionary monetary range within which to select an appropriate amount. Such discretion has occasionally been held to fall exclusively within the province of the judiciary. [*See* Tite v. State Tax Commission, 57 P.2d 734 (Utah 1936)]

c. **Penalties and fines--Texas Association of Business v. Texas Air Control Board,** 852 S.W.2d 440 (Tex. 1993).

   1) **Facts.** The Texas Air Control Board (D) and Water Quality Board (Ds) were administrative agencies created to protect the environment. Neither had power to impose civil penalties for violations of their respective regulations or orders; they had to sue violators in district court. In 1985, how-

Texas Association of Business v. Texas Air Control Board

ever, the legislature granted Ds power to assess civil penalties directly of up to $10,000 per day per violation. The Texas Association of Business (P) brought a declaratory judgment action to have the 1985 statute invalidated. The trial court denied P relief, and P appeals.

2) **Issue.** May a legislature grant an administrative agency the authority to impose civil fines directly without resorting to the courts?

3) **Held.** Yes. Judgment affirmed.

   a) The Texas Constitution preserves a right to trial by jury only for actions tried to a jury at the time the constitution was adopted in 1876. The assessments of environmental penalties by Ds are not actions, or analogous actions, to those tried by jury in 1876.

   b) Trying to compare Ds' actions to common law actions in 1876 is illogical, given the vast difference between the sparsely populated agrarian society of 1876 and the industrialized, environment-threatening society of today. There were simply no governmental regulatory schemes in 1876 that resemble Ds.

   c) This does not mean that the legislature may abrogate the right to trial by jury in any case by delegating duties to an administrative agency.

4) **Concurrence and dissent.** While there is a need to accommodate the evolution of the administrative state, only the narrowest of exceptions to the guarantee of a jury trial should be permitted. Instead, the majority treats trial by jury as a mere anachronism.

## III. INVESTIGATIONS AND INFORMATION

### A. INTRODUCTION

As decisional bodies, agencies require adequate information upon which to base conclusions that best serve legitimate public interest concerns. The means of acquiring such information fall into three categories: (i) requiring reports, (ii) inspection of documents or facilities, and (iii) subpoena of documents and witnesses.

### B. RECORDS AND REPORTS

Many substantive legislative enactments conferring jurisdiction upon administrative agencies include recordkeeping requirements. An agency's authority to secure those records is seldom challenged.

1. **Self-Incrimination.** It has been argued that the Fifth Amendment privilege against self-incrimination prohibits government acquisition of business records.

    a. **Private business records.** In *Shapiro v. United States*, 335 U.S. 1 (1948), the United States Supreme Court held that private business records required to be kept by a fruit and produce wholesaler were not protected by the Fifth Amendment, on grounds that the records involved were the appropriate subjects of governmental regulation, and they were of a kind normally kept in the course of business.

    b. **Records of illegal activities.** But in *Marchetti v. United States*, 390 U.S. 39 (1968), the Supreme Court struck down requirements that gamblers register and file reports regarding their illegal gambling activities, as violating the individual's Fifth Amendment protection against self-incrimination. In distinguishing *Shapiro*, the Court noted that (i) Marchetti was not required to keep records "of the same kind as he has customarily kept," (ii) there were no "public aspects" such records, and (iii) these requirements were directed at a "selective group inherently suspect of criminal activities."

2. **Forced Production of Incriminating Business Records--Craib v. Bulmash,** 777 P.2d 1120 (Cal. 1989).

    a. **Facts.** Bulmash (D) was appointed trustee for his sister and employed attendants to care for her. In response to a complaint that D failed to pay overtime wages, Craib (P), the Deputy Labor Commissioner, served D with a subpoena duces tecum to provide time and wage records for all persons employed by the trust over the previous three-year period. D failed to appear, and P filed a complaint in court to compel production of the documents. The court ordered D to appear before P and produce the records. The court of appeals reversed, relying on the Fourth and Fifth Amendments. P appeals.

b.   **Issue.** May an administrative agency force production of business records required by law to be maintained by the business, even if the records are incriminating?

c.   **Held.** Yes. Judgment reversed.

1)   D cannot claim a Fourth Amendment "privacy" interest in records D is required by lawful statutes or regulations to maintain for the express purpose of agency inspection. These are not his private household records, but business records. So long as the subpoenaed records are relevant to an authorized regulatory purpose and are described with reasonable specificity, an agency's subpoena is not an unreasonable search and seizure.

2)   The Supreme Court has long held that the Fifth Amendment privilege against self-incrimination does not protect against compelled production of records required by law to be kept in order that there may be suitable information of transactions that are the appropriate subjects of governmental regulation and the enforcement of restrictions validly established. The privilege traditionally has not been applied to public records, and records kept in compliance with law have public aspects.

3)   The records P seeks are the appropriate subject of a lawful regulatory scheme. The law encourages voluntary compliance with minimum labor standards designed for the mutual benefit of employees and employers. The standards are enforced not to punish but to ensure that employees have acceptable work environments and that employers who comply are protected against employers who do not comply.

4)   The law requiring maintenance of work records is not directed at activities or persons that are inherently criminal. It applies to every person employing labor in this state, which is hardly a selective or inherently suspect group. The duty to report is triggered by the employment of labor, not the violation of employment laws.

5)   Finally, the law requires only minimal disclosure of information of a kind customarily kept in the ordinary course of business. The information is basic accounting information, and must be regularly summarized in payroll statements provided to employees.

d.   **Concurrence and dissent.** Since the Supreme Court has interpreted the Fifth Amendment to not apply to regulatory agency subpoenas, the court should rely on the state constitution and provide greater protection against self-incrimination. Regulatory agencies should not have a virtually unchallengeable power to enforce their regulations by criminal prosecution based on compelled self-disclosure. If the agencies want to compel disclosure for regulatory purposes, they should be prevented from using the evidence in the prosecution of the individual for any crimes disclosed therein.

## C.  INSPECTIONS

1.  **Warrantless Searches.** The Fourth Amendment prohibition against unreasonable searches and seizures has been interpreted as not to bar warrantless searches of certain highly regulated industries.

2.  **Plain View.** Government officials are free to enter areas open to the public and to take enforcement action based on what they observe in plain view.

3.  **The Exception to the Warrant Requirement for Administrative Searches of Heavily Regulated Industries--New York v. Burger,** 482 U.S. 691 (1987).

    New York
    v. Burger

    a.  **Facts.** Burger (D) owned a junkyard in Brooklyn that was subjected to a warrantless inspection by the New York police. D was arrested after officers found stolen vehicles in his yard. D's motion to suppress the evidence obtained during the inspection was denied by the lower court, but the New York Court of Appeals found that the inspection violated the Fourth Amendment's prohibition against unlawful searches and seizures and reversed. The Supreme Court granted certiorari.

    b.  **Issues.**

        1)  Does this warrantless search fall within the exception to the warrant requirement for administrative inspections of pervasively regulated industries?

        2)  Since the purpose of the search was to deter criminal behavior, is an otherwise proper administrative inspection unconstitutional?

    c.  **Held.** 1) No. 2) No. Judgment reversed.

        1)  The Fourth Amendment's prohibition against warrantless searches and seizures applies to commercial, as well as private, property. An owner and operator of a business has a legitimate expectation of privacy, even with respect to administrative inspections to enforce regulatory statutes.

        2)  However, commercial premises in a closely regulated industry may be subject to a warrantless search so long as (i) there is a substantial government interest, (ii) the search is necessary to

further the regulatory scheme, and (iii) there is a constitutionally adequate substitute for a warrant.

3)   Junkyards are closely regulated businesses in New York and thus there is a reduced expectation of privacy. The state has a substantial interest in prohibiting automotive theft. Regulation of the industry legitimately serves the state's substantial interest in thwarting auto theft. Junkyard owners are on notice that they may be subject to unannounced inspections. Therefore, the search here falls within the exception to the warrant requirement for administrative inspections of closely regulated businesses.

4)   There is no constitutional significance in the fact that police officers, rather than government bureaucrats, conducted the inspection.

## D.   SUBPOENAS

Subpoenas require the giving of information, either in the form of written documents (subpoena duces tecum) or in the form of oral testimony (subpoena ad testificandum).

1.   **Statutory Origins.** For an agency to possess subpoena power, such authority must have a statutory origin. Only courts are free to issue subpoenas without a statutory basis. Most regulatory agencies have been given such power explicitly in their enabling legislation. Even when statutory authority has been vested in the agency head, such power has usually been subdelegated to a subordinate.

2.   **Scope and Effect of Subpoenas.** No agency subpoena has a coercive effect until the judiciary enforces it. However, unlike judicial subpoenas, federal agency subpoenas are ordinarily valid throughout the United States. But again, agencies look to the courts to enforce agency subpoenas.

3.   **APA.** The APA provides that "on contest, the court shall sustain the subpoena or similar process or demand to the extent that it is found to be in accordance with law." [5 U.S.C. §555(d)]

4.   **Pre-Enforcement Challenge to Administrative Subpoena--Texas Lawyers Insurance Exchange v. Resolution Trust Corp.,** 822 F. Supp. 380 (W.D. Tex. 1993).

> Texas Lawyers Insurance Exchange v. Resolution Trust Corp.

a.   **Facts.** The Texas Lawyers Insurance Exchange (P) is a legal malpractice insurance company that insured the law firm of Eikenburg & Stiles, which was a defendant in a lawsuit filed by the Resolution

Trust Corp. (D). D faxed a subpoena duces tecum to P's custodian of records, requesting documents P claimed were privileged as attorney-client communications, attorney work product, and consultant expert reports. P sued in federal court to quash the subpoena. D responded that it could enforce the subpoena only by filing a motion in federal court, so the court has no jurisdiction to consider a pre-enforcement challenge to the subpoena. The case was referred to a United States magistrate.

b. **Issue.** May a federal court exercise jurisdiction over a pre-enforcement challenge to an administrative subpoena when the agency cannot enforce the subpoena without first going to court?

c. **Held.** No. Judgment for D.

1) The Supreme Court held in *Ex Parte Young*, 209 U.S. 123 (1908), that a federal district court has jurisdiction to enjoin enforcement of administrative rates when a party's only other way to contest the rates was to refuse to comply, but the refusal subjected the party to fines and imprisonment. However, in *Reisman v. Caplin*, 375 U.S. 440 (1964), the Court denied jurisdiction for a taxpayer's suit for declaratory and injunctive relief against a subpoena from the Internal Revenue Service ("IRS"), because the IRS could only enforce the subpoena through the courts; *i.e.,* the taxpayer would have a day in court before being subject to penalty.

2) Most other cases have also dismissed pre-enforcement challenges to administrative subpoenas for lack of subject matter jurisdiction.

3) D in this case must resort to judicial enforcement of its subpoenas, so D's subpoena is not self-executing. P's noncompliance with the subpoena prior to judicial action does not subject P to prosecution when the subpoena is attacked in good faith.

d. **Comment.** The district court adopted the magistrate's report in its entirety.

5. **Agency Determines Its Own Jurisdiction--EEOC v. Kloster Cruise Ltd.,** 939 F.2d 921 (11th Cir. 1991).

EEOC v.
Kloster
Cruise Ltd.

a. **Facts.** Kloster Cruise Ltd. (D) was a foreign corporation that owned and operated foreign flagged vessels and had an office in Miami, Florida. Two of D's employees complained to the Equal Employment Opportunity Commission (P) that D had committed employment discrimination against them in violation of Title VII of the Civil Rights Act. P started an investigation and issued two administrative subpoenas duces tecum for evidence relating to D's corporate structure and employment practices. D refused to comply with the subpoenas, and P sought judicial enforcement in district court. The court declined to enforce the subpoenas on the ground that Title VII does not apply to D's cruise ship employees. P appeals.

    **b.**    **Issue.** In an action to enforce an administrative subpoena, may a district court consider the applicability of the particular statute to the parties before it?

    **c.**    **Held.** No. Judgment reversed.

        1)    An agency bringing a subpoena enforcement proceeding need only make a plausible argument supporting jurisdiction; the initial determination of the question of coverage under a particular statute is left to the agency, not the court. Once the agency makes the plausible argument, the court must enforce the subpoena if the information sought is not plainly incompetent or irrelevant to any lawful purpose of the agency.

        2)    In this case, the subpoenas reach documents that would be relevant to jurisdiction, such as whether D's employees were employed by an alter ego of D, how much business D did in Miami, and whether the alleged discrimination occurred in Miami.

        3)    There may be situations where the lack of jurisdiction is so obvious that enforcement would be an abuse of the court's process, but this is not such a situation. D can litigate the issue before P during the administrative hearing process, and then before a court.

FTC v.
American
Tobacco Co.

**6.**    **Fishing Expeditions--FTC v. American Tobacco Co.,** 264 U.S. 298 (1924).

    **a.**    **Facts.** The FTC (P) sought a subpoena requiring the American Tobacco Co. (D) to produce "all letters and telegrams received by the company from, or sent by it to, all of its jobber customers between January 1, 1921 to December 31, 1921, inclusive." P claimed it needed the documents in conjunction with an investigation of the tobacco industry. P appeals from the district court's denial of its petition for enforcement.

    **b.**    **Issue.** Will the courts enforce an administrative agency's subpoena to go on a fishing expedition into private papers on the possibility that they may disclose evidence of crime?

    **c.**    **Held.** No. Judgment affirmed.

        1)    It is contrary to the letter and spirit of the Fourth Amendment and general principles of justice to allow an agency to roam through D's records, "relevant or irrelevant, in the hope that something will turn up."

2) The statute confers the power to obtain such documents as are evidence, not all documents.

3) No general subpoena to engage in a fishing expedition will be issued. Some evidence of materiality of the records sought must be adduced.

4) An administrative agency does not need a case or controversy to inaugurate an investigation. Instead, it is free to investigate merely upon a suspicion that the statute or its regulations are being or has been violated. Hence, its functions are similar to those performed by a grand jury.

    d. **Comment.** The *American Tobacco* doctrine, that fishing expeditions by administrative agencies are not permitted, is no longer the law. In *Endicott Johnson Corp. v. Perkins*, 317 U.S. 501 (1943), the Court held that an agency may conduct an investigation so long as it is of the general kind the agency is authorized to make. In *Oklahoma Press Publishing Co. v. Walling*, 327 U.S. 186 (1946), the Court upheld investigations made for a lawfully authorized purpose. Finally, in *United States v. Morton Salt*, 338 U.S. 632 (1950), the Court permitted requests for information based on official curiosity.

## E. FREEDOM OF INFORMATION → Note 1-6 policies behind FOIA

1. **Introduction.** The Freedom of Information Act ("FOIA"), 5 U.S.C. section 552, amended the APA in 1966 to insist that federal agencies promptly provide requested information unless the information sought falls within one of the nine specific exceptions of section 552(b). The agency has the burden of sustaining its action contrary to the normal presumption that an agency's action is valid.

    a. **Time limits.** Agencies must decide whether to release requested information within 10 working days and decide an appeal of an adverse determination within 20 working days. A 10-day extension may be obtained under "unusual circumstance." [5 U.S.C. §552(a)(6)(B)]

    b. **Segregation.** Even when one of the nine specified exceptions of section 552(b) applies to a portion of the document requested, any reasonably segregable portion thereof that does not fall within the exception shall be provided to the requesting party.

    c. **Judicial review.** FOIA appeals take precedence on the docket of the federal district court, which determines the issues de novo. The agency has the burden of proof to justify its refusal to make the documents available. [5 U.S.C. §552(a)(4)(D)] The courts hold full contempt powers to enforce their determinations, and may assess reasonable attorneys' fees against the government should the complainant prevail. [5 U.S.C. §552(a)(4)(E),(G)] Disciplinary proceedings may be initiated against the agency individual who wrongfully withheld the requested information. The reviewing court is also free, pursuant to the 1974 FOIA amendments, to perform an in camera inspection of the disputed document.

2. **Secrecy Exemption.** The first exemption under FOIA is for matters secret in the interest of national defense and foreign policy which "are in fact properly classified pursuant to executive order." [5 U.S.C. §553(b)(1)(A)] The quoted language was added as a 1974 amendment, largely in order to overrule the decision of *EPA v. Mink*, 410 U.S. 73 (1973).

New York
Times v.
NASA

3. **Exception for Personal Information--New York Times v. NASA,** 920 F.2d 1002 (D.C. Cir. 1990).

   a. **Facts.** NASA (D) refused a FOIA request to release the tape of voice communications aboard the Challenger space shuttle prior to its mid-air explosion on grounds that it constituted "personnel and medical and similar files" within Exemption 6 of the FOIA. It did, however, provide the *New York Times* (P) with a written transcript of the tape. D insisted that releasing the tape would subject the astronauts' families to "an intrusion on their grief which would certainly exacerbate feelings of hurt and loss." P contended that the inflections of the voices would reveal more about what happened during the moments leading to the disaster than the transcript, and that the discussion between the astronauts and NASA Houston contained no personal information about the astronauts and their families. The district court, and a divided panel of the D.C. Circuit, found that the tape did not fall within Exemption 6, and ordered its release.

   b. **Issue.** Does the tape fall within the exception for a "similar file" within Exemption 6 of FOIA?

   c. **Held.** The case is remanded to the district court to determine whether any invasion of the astronauts' privacy, or that of their families, is unwarranted when compared with the citizens' right to be informed. Case remanded.

      1) To qualify as a "similar file" within Exemption 6, the information must contain intimate details about the individual of the same magnitude as that contained in medical and personnel records.

      2) The nature of the file in which the information is contained is not determinative. The issue is whether the information in a file applies to a particular individual.

3) The voices of the astronauts, and whatever they reveal about their thoughts and feelings, constitute information that applies to particular individuals.

4. **Exemption for Personal Information--O'Kane v. U.S. Customs Service,** 169 F.3d 1308 (11th Cir. 1999).

   a. **Facts.** The United States Customs Service (D) refused a FOIA request to release a list of addresses of individuals whose property it had seized. O'Kane (P) wanted the list to solicit clients for his law practice. The district court granted D summary judgment.

   b. **Issue.** Should D release the addresses of persons whose property it has seized?

   c. **Held.** No. Judgment affirmed.

      1) In assessing FOIA decisions, courts must weigh and balance the individual interest in privacy (here, of their home addresses, an important interest) against the public's corresponding right to know.

      2) The Electronic Freedom of Information Act Amendments of 1996, while affirming that the purpose for which the information is sought is irrelevant, nevertheless did not narrow the FOIA's privacy exclusion or erode the balancing test to be used by courts.

      3) Individuals also have a privacy interest in their criminal histories.

5. **Reverse FOIA Litigation.** Information acquired by an administrative agency is often secured under an implicit or explicit promise that the tendered data will remain confidential. But parties who tendered such information have generally been unsuccessful in their attempts to enjoin release thereof by the agency. [*See* Chrysler Corp. v. Brown, 441 U.S. 281 (1979)]

F. **SUNSHINE LAWS**

1. **Government in the Sunshine Act.**

   a. **General rule.** Meetings of a sufficient number of agency members to transact business must be open to the public. [5 U.S.C. §552b(b)]

   b. **Exceptions.** When the agency votes that the public interest so requires, and the matters under discussion fall within one of the 10 specified exceptions, the meetings need not be public. Among the exceptions are discussions of:

(i)     Matters properly classified as secret;

(ii)    Internal personnel rules;

(iii)   Matters exempt from disclosure by statute;

(iv)    Trade secrets and commercial and financial information;

(v)     Discussions involving an individual accused of a crime;

(vi)    Information, the disclosure of which would constitute a clear unwarranted invasion of personal privacy;

(vii)   Investigatory records compiled for law enforcement purposes;

(viii)  Information involving the regulation or supervision of financial institutions;

(ix)    Information, the disclosure of which would lead to financial speculation, endanger the stability of a financial institution, or frustrate implementation of agency action; or

(x)     Matters involving agency issuance of a subpoena or the agency's participation in a judicial proceeding.

[5 U.S.C. §552b(c)]

c.  **Judicial review.** The federal courts have jurisdiction over disputes arising under the Sunshine Act. [5 U.S.C. §552b(h)]

# IV. RULES AND RULEMAKING

## A. TERMINOLOGY AND RULEMAKING

1. **Rulemaking vs. Adjudication.** Rulemaking involves an agency's exercise of its quasi-legislative powers in the promulgation of prospective standards of conduct. Adjudication involves the performance of its quasi-adjudicatory powers, in the resolution of issues that usually involve factual situations occurring at some prior point in time.

2. **Prospective vs. Retroactive Effect.** Rulemaking is prospective in nature. It prescribes future standards of conduct rather than consequences of past conduct. Adjudication ascribes legal obligations based on present or past conduct.

3. **General vs. Individual Focus.** Rulemaking usually impacts the rights of a large number of persons in the abstract. A subsequent proceeding is ordinarily required before an individual will be sanctioned for its violation. Adjudication usually applies immediately to named persons or specific factual situations.

4. **APA Definitions.** The APA provides some rather obscure definitions of rulemaking and adjudication.

   a. **Adjudication.** Adjudication consists of the agency process for the formulation of an "order." [5 U.S.C. §551(7)] An "order" constitutes the final disposition of agency business in a matter other than "rulemaking," but including licensing. [5 U.S.C. §551(b)]

   b. **Rulemaking.** A rule consists of an agency statement of general or particular applicability and future effect designed to implement, interpret or prescribe law or policy. Usually, rulemaking can be identified by:

      1) **General application.** Rulemaking is usually applied generally to all persons who fall within its provisions. This is to be distinguished from an order, which applies immediately to named persons and specific factual situations; and

      2) **Prospective application.** Before a rule is made directly applicable to a named individual, a further proceeding is required. Hence, the rule declares standards for future conduct rather than the consequences of past conduct. Rulemaking is somewhat analogous in this respect to legislation, which is also ordinarily of prospective effect.

   c. **Comment.** Note that the APA definitional scheme identifies adjudication by that which is not rulemaking.

5.  **Confusion in Terminology.** Although an "order" is deemed ordinarily to be the product of adjudication rather than rulemaking, courts have ignored improperly labeled "orders" that result from rulemaking, and instead viewed them as de facto rules. [*See* People v. Cull, 10 N.Y.2d 123 (1961)]

6.  **Procedural Differences.** As we shall see, the procedural obligations for rulemaking are usually "informal," consisting of the disposition of the proceeding on the basis of the written record. The procedural obligations for adjudication are more frequently "formal," or trial-type in nature.

7.  **Types of Rules.** There are four types of rules.

    a.  **Substantive rules.** These are the most significant of the four. They identify appropriate standards of future conduct, and have the force and effect of law.

    b.  **Procedural rules.** These identify the procedural obligations for agency or regulated activity.

    c.  **Housekeeping rules.** These deal with relatively trivial executive-type administrative matters.

    d.  **Interpretative rules.** These clarify or explain existing law, rather than create new law. Standing alone, they do not have the force and effect of law (although the existing law they interpret may).

8.  **Advantages of Rulemaking.**

    a.  Rulemaking shortens and simplifies the administrative process.

    b.  Rulemaking clarifies the law in advance and avoids the retroactive imposition of a new and unexpected liability. Hence, it reduces the impact of new law on settled expectations. It also avoids the problem of obscurity of agency policy that results from case-by-case adjudication.

    c.  Rulemaking offers the agency resource-saving flexibility in fulfilling its responsibilities because ordinarily procedures less cumbersome than a formal trial-type hearing may be employed.

    d.  The use of rulemaking opens up the development of agency policy to a broad range of input from a wide variety of sources that might not be forthcoming in adjudication. It does this by providing constructive notice to the public through publication of notice of proposed rulemaking in the Federal Register. This affords all interested persons an opportunity to respond. By forcing important policy issues into the public arena, the likelihood of more prudent and responsible agency action is enhanced.

*different procedural requirements under ē APA govern, depending on whether ā agency is engaged in rulemaking or adjudication in ā given case.*

e. The availability of notice prior to the promulgation of the rule permits wide public participation. This avoids the problem that often exists in adjudication of singling out one member of an industry for the initial imposition of new and unexpected liability.

9. **Determining What Is a "Rule"--Cordero v. Corbisiero,** 599 N.E.2d 670 (N.Y. 1992).

a. **Facts.** Corbisiero (D), chairman of the New York Racing Board, had a "Saratoga policy" for its Saratoga racetrack, which applied to every jockey who races at Saratoga. The policy required that, following an administrative appeal, a suspension imposed for an infraction committed at the Saratoga racetrack be served at the Saratoga meet the following year. D directed that the policy be applied against Cordero (P). P challenged the policy on the ground that is was a "rule" under the state APA, but was not formally promulgated pursuant to the rulemaking procedures set forth in the state APA. The lower courts denied P relief. The court of appeals granted certiorari.

b. **Issue.** Is an administrative agency's policy a "rule" if it is a general principle applied without regard to the facts and circumstances of the individual case?

*Future effects + general applicability : looks like a rule*

c. **Held.** Yes. Judgment modified.

1) D claims the Saratoga policy merely affects the implementation of a penalty, not the jockey's conduct, and hence is not a rule. However, the policy does not relate to the penalty as such. Instead, it establishes a mandatory procedure that pertains only to when and where a Saratoga suspension must be served in the event of an appeal.

2) The Saratoga policy fits the definition of a rule as an agency's stated policy of general applicability that prescribes a procedure or practice requirement of the agency.

## B. SUBSTANTIVE RULES

Substantive rules prescribe individual rights and duties. They are analogous to statutes, in that they prescribe standards for the future, and their violation may result in the imposition of appropriate sanctions.

1. **Judicial Favor.** In recent years, numerous courts have favored the exercise of rulemaking authority by liberally upholding the statutory foundations therefor, and by encouraging agencies to employ rulemaking as a means of identifying broad legal standards.

**In re
Permanent
Surface
Mining
Regulation
Litigation**

2. **Use of Rulemaking--*In re* Permanent Surface Mining Regulation Litigation,** 653 F.2d 514 (D.C. Cir. 1981).

    a. **Facts.** The Surface Mining Act conferred on the Secretary of the Interior (D) both general and specific rulemaking authority to promulgate regulations designed to minimize the environmental harm resulting from mining operations. D adopted rules prescribing minimum filing requirements for state permit applications pursuant to the general rulemaking authority. Various interested persons (Ps) filed suit in the District Court for the District of Columbia, arguing that the general grant of rulemaking authority was redundant of specific grants, and so the general grant must be limited to rulemaking for housekeeping purposes. The district court ruled for D. Ps appeal.

    b. **Issue.** May a general rulemaking provision serve as the basis for the promulgation of substantive rules?

    c. **Held.** Yes.

*[handwritten margin note: substantive rule making does not exist if the agency's power is not stated in a enabling statute → Not in statute → No agency rulemaking ... always check enabling statute!]*

       1) The courts have willingly upheld substantive regulations based on general rulemaking authority even when specific rulemaking powers exist.

       2) The courts favor rulemaking over adjudication as the more desirable means of developing agency policy, because rulemaking constitutes an efficient and effective means of regulating enterprises subject to agency jurisdiction. *(See pp 227)*

    d. **Comment.** Other courts have also praised the benefits of rulemaking as "allowing the agencies to proceed more expeditiously, give greater certainty and deploy its internal resources more effectively . . . ." [National Petroleum Refiners v. FTC, 482 F.2d 672 (D.C. Cir. 1973)]

**American
Hospital
Association
v. NLRB**

3. **Rulemaking to Guide Adjudications--American Hospital Association v. NLRB,** 499 U.S. 606 (1991).

*[handwritten margin note: Ct skirting case by case language even if req'd to do case by case, agency can still promulgate rules to assist in adjudication]*

    a. **Facts.** The National Labor Relations Board (D) promulgated a substantive rule defining the employee units appropriate for collective bargaining in acute care hospitals. With three exceptions, the rule provided that eight units are appropriate in such hospitals. The American Hospital Association (P) challenged the facial validity of the rule on the ground that the National Labor Relations Act requires D to make a separate bargaining unit determination "in each case" and thus prevents D from using general rules to define bargaining units. The lower courts found for D. The Supreme Court granted certiorari.

**b.** **Issue.** May an administrative agency promulgate a rule regarding the number of collective bargaining units for a specific type of business where the statute requires it to decide in each case what the appropriate collective bargaining unit shall be?

**c.** **Held.** Yes. Judgment affirmed.

1) Among other things, the Act provides that the representative selected for purposes of collective bargaining by the majority of the employees in a unit shall be the exclusive bargaining representative for all the employees in that unit. Thus, the designation of a unit is significant, and the initiative in selecting the appropriate unit resides with the employees.

2) Because of the potential for disagreement regarding the appropriateness of a unit selected by the union seeking recognition, the Act also authorizes D to decide whether the designated unit is appropriate. The Act provides that D "shall decide in each case whether . . . the Unit appropriate for the purposes of collective bargaining shall be the employer unit, craft unit, plant or subdivision thereof."

3) P claims that the phrase "in each case" limits D's rulemaking powers such that D cannot impose any industrywide rule delineating the appropriate bargaining units. A more natural reading indicates that whenever there is a disagreement about the appropriateness of a unit, D shall resolve the dispute. D can resolve disputes with the guidance of its own rules, whether created in the process of case-by-case adjudication or by the exercise of rulemaking authority. Even where the statute requires individualized determinations, the decisionmaker may rely on rulemaking to resolve issues of general applicability unless Congress clearly withholds that authority.

4) D's rule regarding acute care hospitals is not an irrebuttable presumption, as it contains an exception for extraordinary circumstances that provides sufficient flexibility for case-by-case determinations as the need arises.

*powers are not lost even if it is not used.*

5) P also claims the rule is arbitrary and capricious because it ignores critical differences among the acute care hospitals in the United States. Although D had previously noted that the diversity of the health care industry precluded generalizations about the appropriateness of any particular bargaining unit, D cited its experience with acute care hospitals in particular to justify its rule. D's conclusion that most acute care hospitals are similar enough to support a generalized rule regarding the appropriateness of units was based on a reasoned analysis of an extensive record and should be upheld.

**4. Erroneous Statutory Interpretation--Sutton v. United Air Lines,** 527 U.S. 471 (1999).

    **a. Facts.** Twin sisters (Ps) sought employment with United Airlines (D) as pilots. Both suffered from severe myopia, and were denied employment because they failed to meet the company's requirement of 20/100 uncorrected vision. Ps brought suit under the Americans With Disabilities Act ("ADA") on grounds they were discriminated against because of their disability. D argued that Ps did not fall under the ADA since their corrected vision did not qualify as a disability under the statute. However, the Equal Employment Opportunity Commission ("EEOC") had promulgated regulations providing that, in determining whether an individual possesses a disability within the meaning of the act, they are to be assessed without regard to mitigating measures. Ps' complaint was dismissed for failure to state a claim upon which relief could be granted.

    **b. Issue.** Does the applicability of the ADA require an assessment of a disability without regard to mitigating measures?

*Ct wanted to make clear that this was not Congress's Intent*

    **c. Held.** No. The EEOC's interpretation of the statute is erroneous. Judgment affirmed.

        1) One falls within the protection of the ADA only if one suffers from a disability that cannot be corrected. Here, glasses or contact lenses could correct Ps' myopia; therefore, they did not fall under the ADA.

        2) No agency has been given authority to interpret the provisions of the ADA in question. The EEOC's interpretation is impermissible and contrary to congressional intent. Congress did not intend to bring under the ADA persons whose uncorrected conditions amounted to disabilities.

**C. LEGAL EFFECT** *→See PP 242 7 factors of legislative rule.*

    **1. General Rule.** Regulations that are properly promulgated and within the scope of the authority delegated have the force and effect of law. Stated differently, a rule or regulation has the same effect as the statute on which it is based, as long as the rule or regulation is not ultra vires of jurisdiction conferred by the statute, and as long as its method of promulgation does not suffer from procedural infirmities.

    **2. Housekeeping and Procedural Rules.** The principle that a properly promulgated rule has the same effect as a statute applies not only to substantive rules, but to housekeeping and procedural rules as well. Indeed, many courts have held that an agency is obligated to afford parties all the procedures identified in their procedural regulations, even though they exceed the requirement of the underlying statute or the Constitution.

3.  **Interpretive Rules.** In contrast to substantive regulations, interpretive rules do not have the force and effect of law. While they may explain the agency's interpretation of its enabling statute, they are normally not deemed binding on either the agency or persons subject to its jurisdiction. However, many courts view them as persuasive authority in interpreting the statutes to which they relate.

4.  **Agency's Compliance with Its Own Rules--Reuters Ltd. v. FCC,** 781 F.2d 946 (D.C. Cir. 1986).

    Reuters Ltd. v. FCC

    a.  **Facts.** The FCC (D) approved an application by Reuters Ltd. (P) for 13 microwave radio station licenses. On the same day, a competitor, Associated, submitted applications for the same channels. However, they were filed in the wrong office, so that when P was awarded the licenses, no competing applications had been filed. Associated protested the grant to P, claiming D had improperly granted the licenses before the 60-day period established by D itself had expired. While one of D's pronouncements indicated a 60-day period would be permitted, another authorized award of a license after a 30-day period. D found for Associated, but P appealed to the full FCC, which held that despite the correctness of P's technical legal arguments, fairness required that Associated be permitted to compete for the licenses. P appeals to federal court.

    b.  **Issue.** If an agency issues confusing pronouncements as to the time constraints in awarded licenses, may it resort to fairness in revoking a properly granted license in order to allow a misled competitor to compete for the license?

    c.  **Held.** No. Judgment for P.

        *Properly enacted regulations have a force of law.*

        1)  D admits that although its subjective intent was not to guarantee a 60-day filing period, its pronouncements may have been misleading to prospective licensees such as Associated. However, D's understandable attempt to do justice is not permissible.

        2)  D properly granted the licenses to P pursuant to its rules. An agency must adhere to its own rules and regulations. It cannot occasionally depart from its rules to do what it considers to be justice. Rules are rules. D interpreted its rules in the manner asserted by P and the courts cannot permit an agency to deviate from its rules.

        *Ad hoc departures from those rules, even to achieve laudable aims, cannot be sanctioned.*

5.  **Retroactivity--Bowen v. Georgetown University Hospital,** 488 U.S. 204 (1988).

    Bowen v. Georgetown University Hospital

    a.  **Facts.** The Medicare Act and the Social Security Amendments of 1972 authorized the Secretary of Health and Human Services to promulgate regulations setting limits on the levels of Medicare costs that private health care providers will be reimbursed for. Bowen (D), the Secretary, issued cost-limit schedules on an annual basis. In 1981, D issued a cost-limit schedule that included technical changes to various calculations, including the wage index used to calculate salary levels for hospital employees in different parts of the country. Georgetown University Hospital and others (Ps) sued to have the 1981 schedule held invalid. The district court found that D violated the APA by not providing notice and opportunity for public comment before issuing the rule. Rather than appeal, D applied the pre-1981 wage-index method. In 1984, D published a notice for public comment on a proposal to reissue the 1981 wage-index rule, retroactive to 1981. Because Congress had in the meantime established different cost reimbursement procedures, the effect of the proposed change would be to apply the method to a 15-month period starting in 1981. The rule was implemented, and D started collecting overpayments from the hospitals involved. Ps as a group were required to reimburse D for over $2 million. The district court invalidated the retroactive application of the rule, and the court of appeals affirmed. The Supreme Court granted certiorari.

b.    **Issue.** May an administrative agency apply rules retroactively?

c.    **Held.** No. Judgment affirmed.

1)    Any federal administrative agency's power to promulgate legislative regulations is limited to the authority delegated by Congress. Thus, D could have power to impose the rule retroactively only if Congress granted that power.

2)    Retroactivity is not favored in the law, and the courts require express language from Congress regarding such power. D notes that the Medicare Act provides both a specific grant of authority to promulgate regulations to provide for suitable retroactive corrective adjustments, and a general grant of authority to promulgate cost-limit rules.

3)    While D has authority to make retroactive corrective adjustments, D has in the past interpreted this to refer to a year-end balancing of the monthly installments received by a provider with the aggregate due it for the year. It was never meant to support the retroactive change of a rule. And Congress clearly never expressly authorized retroactive cost-limit rules.

d.    **Concurrence** (Scalia, J.). The APA's definition of a rule refers to its future effect; a "rule" is a statement that has legal consequences only for the future. While Congress could retroactively change its laws, it does not have to delegate this to the agencies, although it can.

6. **Other Types of Rules--La Casa del Convaleciente v. Sullivan,** 965 F.2d 1175 (1st Cir. 1992).

    a. **Facts.** The Secretary of Health and Human Services announced a new "gap filling" reimbursement system for suppliers of durable medical equipment under the Medicare system. Notice and comment procedures were not used. The district court held that they need not be used because the agency action was an interpretive rule, not a substantive rule, and thus not subject to the APA's notice-and-comment procedural requirements.

    b. **Issue.** Is the system in question an interpretive rule for which notice and comment procedures are not required?

    c. **Held.** Yes. Judgment affirmed.

        1) Substantive rules have the force and effect of law, and must be issued only after notice and comment procedures.

        2) Interpretive rules merely clarify or explain existing statutes or rules, and need only be announced, without notice and comment procedures.

        3) The agency's own characterization of the issue is important, but not determinative.

        4) When a complex scheme of Medicare reimbursement is at issue, the agency is entitled to heightened deference.

## D. COST-BENEFIT ANALYSIS

1. **Strict Cost-Benefit Approach Rejected--American Textile Manufacturers Institute v. Donovan,** 452 U.S. 490 (1981).

    a. **Facts.** Following passage of the Occupational Safety and Health Act of 1970, safety standards were established under section 6(a) of the Act for exposure to cotton dust generated by the preparation and manufacture of cotton products. Inhalation of the dust caused byssinosis, or "brown lung" disease. In 1978, permanent standards were established of 200 to 750 micrograms per cubic meter of air averaged over an eight-hour workday (depending on the segment of the cotton industry). The American Textile Manufacturers Institute (P) challenged the validity of the standards on the ground that the 1970 Act requires OSHA to demonstrate that the standard reflects a reasonable relationship between the costs and benefits associated therewith. The lower court held that the Act does not require such a comparison.

**b.** **Issue.** Does the Occupational Safety and Health Act of 1970 require a determination that the costs of a standard bear a reasonable relationship to its benefits?

**c.** **Held.** No. Judgment affirmed.

1) Significantly, section 6(b)(5) of the Act merely requires that the standard ensure employees' health and safety "to the extent feasible." By the plain meaning of the word "feasible," Congress has indicated its decision that workers' health and safety must outweigh all considerations save those which make this goal unattainable. When Congress deems a cost-benefit analysis to be sufficient, it so specifies in the statute; however, here it did not do so.

2) P argues that the general definition of an occupational safety and health standard contained in section 3(8) of the Act engrafts a cost-benefit analysis requirement onto section 6(b)(5) by stating that the standard must be "reasonably necessary or appropriate." However, this interpretation would effectively eviscerate section 6(b)(5), and it would be illogical to assume that this was Congress's intent.

3) The legislative history of the Act supports the interpretation that Congress intended to impose a feasibility, not a cost-benefit, analysis on standards promulgated thereunder.

*In re* Dravo Basic Materials Co., Inc.

**2.** **Quantification Not Required to Conduct Cost-Benefit Analysis--*In re Dravo Basic Materials Co., Inc.,* 604 So. 2d 630 (La. Ct. App. 1992).**

**a.** **Facts.** Dravo Basic Materials Co., Inc. (P) applied for water discharge permits necessary to conduct shell dredging in Lake Pontchartrain. An administrative law judge held a three-week adjudicatory hearing and reported his findings of fact and conclusions of law to the Office of Water Resources in the Department of Environmental Quality ("DEQ"). The assistant secretary of the office reviewed P's application and the hearing record and, determining that shell dredging could not be undertaken in a manner that would adequately protect the environment, denied P's application. P appeals, claiming the assistant secretary's findings did not contain a cost-benefit analysis.

**b.** **Issue.** When an agency is required to conduct a cost-benefit analysis, must it quantify all relevant considerations?

**c.** **Held.** No. Judgment affirmed.

1) The Louisiana Supreme Court has required the DEQ to consider whether potential and real adverse environmental effects of a proposed activity have been avoided to the maximum extent possible, whether a cost-benefit analysis of the environmental impact costs

outweigh the social and economic benefits of the activity, and whether there are alternative projects that would offer more protection to the environment. [*See* Save Ourselves, Inc. v. Louisiana Environmental Control Commission, 452 So. 2d 1152 (La. 1984)]

    2)    At the hearing, P submitted evidence of the substantial economic benefits of shell dredging and the harsh economic impacts of closing the industry. Environmental groups offered evidence that P's experts did not consider the "opportunity costs" of allowing shell dredging. Some of these could be quantified in recreational, tourism, and other benefits, but harm to the environment cannot be so quantified.

    3)    The *Save Ourselves* case does not require the DEQ to explain its cost-benefit analysis in detail, so long as the analysis is done. The assistant secretary's judgment that the environmental costs outweigh the social and economic benefits is not clearly erroneous, and she was not arbitrary and capricious in making her decision, so it must be upheld.

## E.  PUBLICATION

  **1.**  **Federal Register.** Since 1955, federal law has insisted that all federal agency rules and regulations be printed in the Federal Register, which is published every working day. Such publication is a condition precedent to the legal effectiveness of any rule or regulation, unless the parties affected have actual knowledge thereof.

  **2.**  **Code of Federal Regulations.** The Code of Federal Regulations is an annual, indexed compilation of all federal rules and regulations promulgated. Hence, once the rule or regulation becomes final, it is ordinarily published in the annual volumes of the Code of Federal Regulations.

  **3.**  **Effect of Publication.** The proper publication of federal agency rules and regulations results in constructive notice to the world. All persons to whom such regulations apply are bound by their provisions irrespective of whether they have actual knowledge of the rules' existence. Contradictory information supplied by a federal official does not alter the strict language of a properly published rule or regulation.

  **4.**  **Erroneous Information--Federal Crop Insurance Corp. v. Merrill,** 332 U.S. 380 (1947).

> Federal Crop Insurance Corp. v. Merrill
>
> + Reuters case

    **a.**  **Facts.** Merrill and other Idaho wheat farmers (Ps) sought insurance proceeds from the Federal Crop Insurance Corp. (D) for destruction of their crops by drought. Ps had been erroneously informed by D's employees that their crops were insurable; in fact, new regulations had recently been published in the Federal Register that disqualified Ps. Ps won a verdict in the lower Idaho court, which was affirmed by the Idaho Supreme Court. D appeals to the United States Supreme Court.

b. **Issue.** Since assurances given by an agent bind a private insurance company, does erroneous information conferred by a federal agency official bind the agency?

c. **Held.** No. Judgment reversed.

1) Just as "ignorance of the law is no excuse" with respect to statutes, the same principle applies to regulations. This is true even where the agency's official is apparently unaware of the regulation.

5. **States.** Most states have specified a central state office for the filing of all state regulations and have provided for their periodic compilation and publication. But no state follows the federal approach of requiring daily publication of agency rules and regulations.

### F. EXCURSUS ON ESTOPPEL

1. **General Rule.** Erroneous or unauthorized advice given by an agency official that contradicts a binding regulation is usually insufficient grounds upon which to sustain a case of estoppel against the government.

Office of
Personnel
Management
v. Richmond

2. **Estoppel in Favor of the Government--Office of Personnel Management v. Richmond,** 496 U.S. 414 (1990).

a. **Facts.** Richmond (P) was on disability retirement as a former federal employee. His disability payments were subject to termination in the event that he was restored to earning capacity, defined as earning income at least 80% of what he was paid prior to retirement. Prior to 1982, the relevant measuring period for restoration of earning capacity was two succeeding calendar years. In 1982, this was changed to any one calendar year. P had an opportunity to work overtime at his part time job, which put him over the 80% threshold. He sought advice from an employee of the Office of Personnel Management (D), who incorrectly advised P according to the pre-1982 rules. Accordingly, P worked overtime for two consecutive years and lost his disability benefits when the new rule was applied. P appealed the denial of his benefits to the Merit Systems Protection Board, which denied the appeal on the ground that D could not be estopped from enforcing a statutorily imposed requirement. The court of appeals reversed. The Supreme Court granted certiorari.

**b. Issue.** May the government be estopped from enforcing a statutory provision limiting benefit payments when a benefit claimant loses benefits after relying on the erroneous advice of a government employee?

**c. Held.** No. Judgment reversed.

    1) Traditionally, equitable estoppel has not been available to private litigants in suits against the government. Dicta in some Supreme Court opinions may have suggested that equitable estoppel could arise, and although no case has decided that, many claims have been asserted in the lower courts. Still, this case may be decided without holding that no estoppel claim could ever succeed against the federal government.

    2) The Appropriations Clause of the Constitution specifies that only Congress can permit payment of money from the Treasury. P has not met the statutory requirements for payment of the benefits he seeks; the Constitution therefore prohibits that any money be drawn from the Treasury to pay those benefits.

    3) No decision of the Court has upheld an estoppel claim against the government for payment of money. The Appropriations Clause is an important protection against fraud and corruption. If the government could be forced to pay money based on statements and decision of government agents instead of based on Acts of Congress, the Appropriations Clause would become a nullity. The Executive Branch could give claimants erroneous advice and thereby commit federal funds not authorized by Congress.

    4) In difficult cases such as these, relief is available only through Congress; the courts cannot spend federal funds. This has been the basis for "private bills," which Congress has reviewed at the United States Claims Court but still enacts itself.

**d. Concurrence** (Stevens, J.). This case involves a dispute over the rules that govern administration of the appropriation, not whether the appropriation itself has been made. In a more egregious case, the Court could construe the statute to nullify a forfeiture, consistent with congressional intent.

**e. Comment.** Under the APA, parties may secure binding advice from a federal agency. [5 U.S.C. §554(e)] However, the issuance of a declaratory ruling is discretionary with the agency.

## G. RULEMAKING PROCEDURE

Section 553 of the APA defines the procedural obligations applicable to most rulemaking proceedings.

1. **Notice.** Notice of proposed rulemaking must be published in the Federal Register, unless relevant parties have actual notice. [5 U.S.C. §553(b)]

    a. **Exceptions.** Interpretive and procedural rules, a well as general statements of policy, are exempt from the requirement of publication. Also exempt are situations where the agency finds it "impracticable, unnecessary, or contrary to the public interest." [5 U.S.C. §553(b)(3)]

2. **Notice-and-Comment Procedures.** Parties have a right to participate through submission of written pleadings, with or without the opportunity to advocate their position or introduce evidence orally. More formal procedures are available only if the "rules are required to be made on the record after opportunity for an agency hearing. . . ." [5 U.S.C. §553(c)]

3. **Publication.** Publication or service of a substantive rule must ordinarily be accomplished 30 days prior to its effective date.

4. **APA Is Both a Ceiling and a Floor.** In reviewing procedures offered by an agency under the APA, courts are ordinarily not free to impose procedural requirements beyond those specified in the APA. Nor may agencies offer less than the procedural minimums expressed therein. But an agency is free (without judicial coercion) to offer more than the minimum procedural requirements if it so chooses.

5. **Leading Case--Vermont Yankee Nuclear Power Corp. v. Natural Resources Defense Council,** 435 U.S. 519 (1978).

    a. **Facts.** Vermont Yankee Nuclear Power Corp. (D) and other public utilities sought permits from the Atomic Energy Commission ("AEC") to build nuclear power facilities as early as 1967. The Natural Resources Defense Council (P) objected to the issuance of a license, and hearings were held thereon in 1971. In 1972, the AEC instituted rulemaking proceedings to assess the environmental consequences surrounding the spent fuel cycle. The AEC did not offer the opportunity for formal, trial-type proceedings under APA sections 556 and 557, but appeared to offer more than the de minimis procedures specified in the rulemaking provision. [APA §553] The lower courts nevertheless concluded that the procedures offered were inadequate. Ds appeal.

    b. **Issue.** May the judiciary insist that federal agencies offer procedures beyond those expressed in the APA where the substantive issues under consideration are complex, technical, or involve "issues of great public import"?

    c. **Held.** No. Judgment reversed.

        1) The APA expresses the maximum procedural requirements that Congress was willing to have the judiciary place upon agencies. While

Vermont Yankee Nuclear Power Corp. v. Natural Resources Defense Council agencies are free to offer greater procedural opportunities, the courts are not free to insist that they do.

2) Exceptions may exist when:

a) The agency is deciding a controversy involving a small number of persons, each exceptionally affected upon individual grounds (this is essentially a *Londoner*-type of situation, *see infra*);

b) The agency makes a "totally unjustified departure from settled agency procedures of long standing";

c) Constitutional due process may require more procedural opportunities than those specified in the APA; or

d) Exceptionally compelling circumstances exist.

d. **Comment.** *Vermont Yankee* is among the most significant and most frequently cited decisions in administrative law. The courts have generally followed the restriction against imposing rulemaking procedures beyond those required by statute, but this has not prevented the courts from carefully reviewing agency procedures for conformity with the APA requirements.

6. **Presumption in Favor of Informal Rulemaking.** Courts do not ordinarily construe an agency's statutory language identifying procedural obligations for rulemaking to be synonymous with the "on the record" language of APA section 553(c), which would trigger the formal procedures expressed in APA sections 556 and 557. Although a statute does not have to quote section 553 to require formal rulemaking, there must be a clear expression of congressional intent to do so. Otherwise, the courts will assume that Congress intended the agency to conduct informal rulemaking. The rationale is that formal rulemaking is a costly process that does not add much to the agency's ability to make good decisions.

a. **"After hearing" not synonymous with "on the record"--United States v. Florida East Coast Railway,** 410 U.S. 224 (1973).

> United States
> v. Florida
> East Coast
> Railway

1) **Facts.** The Interstate Commerce Commission (D) promulgated "incentive per diem" rules designed to provide an economic incentive for railroads to promptly return boxcars to their owners. The Interstate Commerce Act provides, inter alia, that the ICC "may, after hearing," promulgate various rules affecting rail transportation, including the use of boxcars. The procedures used by D in promulgating the incentive rules somewhat exceeded those specified in APA section 553 for informal rulemaking, but were somewhat less than the formal rulemaking procedures identified in APA sections 556

and 557. The Florida East Coast Railway (P) challenged the rules on grounds that formal procedures should have been utilized. The district court held the rules invalid. D appeals.

2) **Issue.** Is the "after hearing" language of the Interstate Commerce Act essentially synonymous with the "on the record" language of APA section 553(c) so as to require full formal procedures?

3) **Held.** No. Judgment reversed.

a) The words "on the record" of APA section 553(c) are not words of art. Often statutory language having the same meaning could trigger the provisions of sections 556 and 557 in rulemaking proceedings.

b) The APA supplements other legislation. It neither limits nor repeals additional procedural requirements to those specified in the APA, such as those imposed by the "after hearing" language at issue here. [5 U.S.C. §559]

c) The meaning of a term such as "hearing" will vary depending upon whether it is found in the context of statutory provisions involving adjudication or rulemaking. If the former, it is more likely that formal procedures will be required. If the latter, it is a rare case in which formal procedures will be mandated.

d) Even the modest procedural hurdles of APA section 553 do not apply to interpretive rules, general statements of policy, or procedural rules, or when the agency for good cause finds that notice and public procedure thereon are impracticable, unnecessary, or contrary to the public interest.

e) Even if APA sections 556 and 557 are triggered because the rulemaking statute is interpreted to require APA section 553(c) "on the record" procedures, nevertheless APA section 556(d) allows the submission of the evidence in written form if the parties will not be "prejudiced thereby."

4) **Comment.** Although at least 15 federal statutes use the specific language "on the record" when describing the procedures to be utilized for rulemaking (thereby triggering APA sections 556 and 557), most do not. Nevertheless, courts do occasionally conclude that other statutory language is essentially synonymous with the "on the record" requirement.

7. **Prejudgment.** Although prejudgment bias constitutes grounds for disqualification of the decisionmaker when quasi-judicial procedures are mandated,

neutrality and detached objectivity are not strictly insisted upon in quasi-legislative proceedings.

a. **Agency official's public expression of opinion on the issue--Association of National Advertisers v. FTC,** 617 F.2d 1151 (D.C. Cir. 1979).

1) **Facts.** The FTC (D) proposed rules restricting children's advertising on television. The chairman of the FTC had made public statements regarding the regulation. The Association of National Advertisers (P) asked that D's chairman recuse himself from the rulemaking proceeding, but he refused. P sued to have D's chairman disqualified. The district court found that the chairman had prejudged issues of fact and granted P's motion for summary judgment. D appeals.

2) **Issue.** Must an agency official be enjoined from participating in his agency's rulemaking proceeding if he has publicly expressed an opinion on the issues that are the subject of the proceeding?

3) **Held.** No. Judgment reversed.

a) The district court relied on *Cinderella Career & Finishing Schools, Inc. v. FTC*, 425 F.2d 583 (D.C. Cir. 1970), which held that the standard for disqualifying an administrator in an adjudicatory proceeding because of prejudgment is whether a disinterested observer may conclude that the administrator has in some measure adjudged the facts as well as the law of a particular case in advance of hearing it. This ensures an impartial decisionmaker for an adjudicative hearing.

b) The district court determined that D's pending rulemaking proceeding in this case had adjudicative aspects that made *Cinderella* applicable. However, administrative action under the APA is either adjudication or rulemaking; it cannot be a hybrid. While there are specific statutory procedures that apply to D's proceeding that exceed the normal procedures required for rulemaking, the nature of the proceeding is still rulemaking because it is directed to all members of an affected industry and is based on legislative fact.

c) There are no judicially-imposed procedural requirements on legislatures, and legislators are even expected to prejudge factual and policy issues. Due process does not demand procedures for rulemaking that are more rigorous than those specified by Congress. The *Cinderella* rule does not apply to rulemaking.

d) Administrators in rulemaking proceedings must be impartial, but this does not mean they must be uninformed or without opinions. A rulemaker may not be disqualified unless there is a clear and convincing showing that he has an unalterably closed mind on matters critical to the disposition of the rulemaking. P did not make such a showing in this case.

## H.  RULES VS. ORDERS

1.  **General Rule.** An administrative agency is free to apply a new principle retroactively in an adjudicatory proceeding. It need not utilize rulemaking as a sole means of announcing new policy on a prospective basis. [*See* SEC v. Chenery Corp., 332 U.S. 194 (1947)]

2.  **Rulemaking Through Adjudication--NLRB v. Wyman-Gordon Co.,** 394 U.S. 759 (1969).

    a.  **Facts.** In ordering a union election at the facilities of Wyman-Gordon Co. (D), the NLRB (P) ordered D to provide the unions with a list of the names and addresses of eligible electors. D refused to supply the list, and the unions lost their elections. P ordered a second election, and D again refused to provide the list. P had announced the list requirement prospectively in its prior adjudication. [Excelsior Underwear, Inc., 156 N.L.R.B. 1236 (1966)] P sought an order from the district court to enforce its subpoena. The district court granted the order. The court of appeals reversed. P appeals.

    b.  **Issue.** May an administrative agency issue a new and binding rule prospectively in the context of an adjudication without utilizing rulemaking procedures?

    c.  **Held.** No. Judgment reversed on other grounds.

        1)  In *Excelsior*, the NLRB purported to establish a general rule but declined to apply the rule to the parties before it in the *Excelsior* adjudication. However, in order to announce a new rule prospectively, it was incumbent on the NLRB to comply with the rulemaking procedures of APA section 553. Since the NLRB did not do this, *Excelsior* was void as a vehicle for the establishment of a new rule. Nevertheless, the NLRB in the Wyman-Gordon adjudication had issued an order insisting that D supply a list, and despite the fact that it erroneously cited *Excelsior*, the order itself established an obligation to provide the list.

    d.  **Concurrence** (Black, Brennan, Marshall, JJ.). The *Excelsior* rule was properly adopted, and hence was binding in all future cases. The majority opinion forces agencies either unfairly to impose new obligations retroactively upon parties to the adjudication, or abandon the effort temporarily and inaugurate a separate rulemaking proceeding.

NLRB v. Wyman-Gordon Co.

e.    **Dissent** (Douglas, J.). If the NLRB treated every case on its special facts, we could affirm this case, but instead it followed a different course in *Excelsior.* The rule in *Excelsior* should have been put down for a public hearing.

f.    **Dissent** (Harlan, J.). An agency is not "adjudicating" when it announces a rule that it refuses to apply to the dispute before it. Instead it is making a rule.

g.    **Comment.** Modern courts appear to encourage rulemaking over adjudication as a vehicle for announcing new policy, although most courts still defer to the agency's discretion as to which means it will employ.

## I.   LEGISLATIVE REVIEW

1.    **Legislative Veto.** The congressional (or legislative) veto is a means by which the Congress, or either House, can implement new policy, or reverse administrative agency initiatives, without subjecting congressional action to the presidential veto provisions of Article I, Section 7 of the United States Constitution.

2.    **Methods.** The legislative veto can be exercised to reverse administrative agency action when the substantive statute governing the agency's actions requires submission of the proposed agency rule or order to Congress for legislative approval or disapproval prior to its effectiveness. The following alternatives exist:

a.    **Either house disapproves.** The proposed action can be precluded if either House of Congress passes a resolution explicitly disapproving the agency action within a specified time;

b.    **Both houses disapprove.** The statute can require that both the Senate and House of Representatives reject, by majority vote, the proposed agency action;

c.    **Either house approves.** The statute can allow the agency action to go into effect if either house approves it;

d.    **Both houses approve.** If both the Senate and House approve the agency action, it becomes effective; or

e.    **Committee approval or disapproval.** Legislative veto authority has, on occasion, been vested in a committee of one or both houses.

3.    **Popularity.** The first federal legislative veto provision was enacted in 1932. Since then, Congress adopted 295 congressional veto provisions in 196 separate statutes. Their popularity grew significantly between 1970 and 1983, when the *Chadha* case was decided (*see* below).

**4. Unconstitutionality--INS v. Chadha,** 462 U.S. 919 (1983).

    **a.** **Facts.** Chadha (P) was an East Indian who lawfully entered the United States on a nonimmigrant student visa. After his visa expired, the Immigration and Naturalization Service (D) held a deportation hearing. The immigration judge suspended P's deportation and sent a report to Congress as required by section 244(c)(1) of the Immigration and Naturalization Act. Section 244(c)(2) provided that either House of Congress could veto a suspension of deportation. The House of Representatives adopted a unilateral resolution opposing P's permanent residence, and P was ordered deported. P sought review in the Ninth Circuit, which held section 244(c)(2) unconstitutional. The Supreme Court granted certiorari.

    **b.** **Issue.** May Congress employ the legislative veto device to oversee delegation of its constitutional authority to the executive branch?

    **c.** **Held.** No. Judgment affirmed.

        1) Although this case has political ramifications, it is primarily a constitutional challenge, which presents a bona fide controversy, properly subject to judicial action.

        2) Article I of the Constitution vests all legislative powers in both Houses of Congress. Every bill or resolution must be passed by both Houses and approved by the President (or his veto overridden) before it takes effect. These provisions are intended to secure liberty through separation of powers. The bicameral nature of Congress similarly ensures careful consideration of all legislation.

        3) The action taken by the House in this case was essentially legislative in purpose and effect. The legislative veto replaced the constitutional procedure of enacting legislation requiring P's deportation (a private bill). Yet the Constitution enumerates only four instances in which either House may act alone: (i) impeachment, (ii) trial after impeachment, (iii) ratification of treaties, and (iv) confirmation of presidential appointments. The legislative veto is not enumerated.

        4) Although the legislative veto may be efficient, efficiency is not the overriding value behind the Constitution. Separation of powers, as set up by the Constitution, may not be eroded for convenience. Therefore, the legislative veto is unconstitutional. Once Congress delegates authority, it must abide by that delegation until it legislatively alters or revokes it.

    **d.** **Dissent** (White, J.). The legislative veto is a valid response to the dilemma of choosing between no delegation (and hence no lawmaking because of the vast amount of regulation necessary under our system) and abdication of the lawmaking function to the executive branch and administrative agencies. The legislative veto has been included in nearly 200 statutes, accepted by presidents for 50 years, and allows resolution of major constitutional and policy differences between Congress and the president. Because the underlying legislation was properly enacted, and because the Constitution does not prohibit it, the legislative veto is constitutional.

## J. NEGOTIATED RULEMAKING = does not replace notice + comment rulemaking

1. **Negotiated Rulemaking--USA Group Loan Services v. Riley,** 82 F.3d 708 (7th Cir. 1996).

   a. **Facts.** In its 1992 Amendments to the Higher Education Act, Congress required the Department of Education (D) to enter into a "negotiated rulemaking" process before promulgating any final rules. Under this process, the Secretary of Education was to submit draft regulations to affected parties, and negotiate with them over the form and substance of the regulations. USA Group Loan Services and other student loan servicers (Ps) disagreed with proposed provisions making student loan servicers jointly and severally liable with lenders, guarantors, and educational institutions for violations of the federal student loan program. D did indeed undertake negotiations with Ps, during which one of D's officials promised to abide by any consensus reached unless there were compelling reasons to depart. At one point in the negotiations, D offered to cap Ps' liability, an offer that was rejected, and subsequently revoked. Ps argued that D negotiated in bad faith, and that they should be allowed discovery of D's negotiating process. The district court upheld D's position.

   b. **Issue.** Did D conduct negotiated rulemaking in bad faith?

   c. **Held.** No. Judgment affirmed.

      1) The purpose of the negotiated rulemaking process is to reduce judicial challenge to regulations by encouraging the parties to compromise on their differences prior to the formal rulemaking procedure.

      2) It is unclear that D could lawfully agree to be bound by the consensus results of the negotiations.

      3) It is not bad faith for a negotiator to revoke an unaccepted offer.

USA Group
Loan Services
v. Riley

4)   Allowing discovery would unduly prolong the administrative process in contravention of the purpose of Congress in promulgating the negotiated rulemaking process.

## K.   RULEMAKING AND THE INTERNET

There are numerous benefits to negotiated rulemaking (*e.g.*, reduction of judicial challenge, more expeditious rule implementation, more economical process), and these can be enhanced by agencies that post their advanced notices of proposed rulemaking on the Internet, allowing the public to comment on or question the proposed rules.

# V. RIGHT TO BE HEARD

## A. PROCEDURAL DUE PROCESS

1. **Constitution.** The Fifth and Fourteenth Amendments to the United States Constitution insist that no person may be deprived of "life, liberty, or property, without due process of law."

2. **Components.** The essential components of due process are notice and an opportunity to be heard. Notice is ordinarily a simpler question for legal resolution than is the issue of whether an aggrieved party has been accorded a sufficient opportunity to be heard. The fundamental issue is frequently how much process is "due."

## B. LEGISLATIVE VS. JUDICIAL FUNCTIONS

1. **Formal Hearing Required.** The Supreme Court has recognized that a formal hearing is required when there is a "relatively small number of persons, who were exceptionally affected, in each case upon individual grounds. . . ." In *Londoner v. Denver*, 210 U.S. 373 (1908), a case involving the assessment of a tax imposed upon individual property owners for the benefit realized from the paving of their street, the Court held that at some time before the tax becomes irrevocably fixed, the taxpayers must be given the opportunity to have a hearing.

2. **Informal Hearing Sufficient.** The Supreme Court has also held that, conversely, when a large number of persons are affected by an agency action essentially analogous to that performed by the legislature, a formal hearing is not required.

   a. **Increase in value of all taxable property--Bi-Metallic Investment Co. v. Colorado,** 239 U.S. 441 (1915).

      1) **Facts.** Bi-Metallic Investment Co. (P) owned real estate in Denver, and sought to enjoin the State Board of Equalization (D) from increasing the valuation of all taxable property in the city by 40%. P argued that since it was given no opportunity to be heard, its constitutional right to due process had been violated. The Supreme Court of Colorado upheld the revaluation. P appeals.

      2) **Issue.** Do all property owners in a municipality have a right to be heard before their property can be revalued?

      3) **Held.** No. Judgment affirmed.

         a) When a large number of individuals are affected by agency action, it is impractical that they each be given a hearing.

The machinery of government would grind to a halt if all aggrieved parties were given a formal hearing.

     b)    The action taken here was analogous to that regularly performed by the legislature. Even though the legislature can significantly affect the property of individuals "sometimes to the point of ruin," there is no constitutional requirement that a hearing be held before such action is taken.

**3.** ***Londoner* and *Bi-Metallic*.** These decisions illustrate the fundamental distinctions between adjudication and rulemaking. As the Supreme Court has subsequently noted, there is "a recognized distinction in administrative law between proceedings for the purpose of promulgating policy-type rules or standards, on the one hand, and proceedings designed to adjudicate disputed facts in particular cases on the other." The distinction is aptly illustrated by the landmark decisions of *Londoner* and *Bi-Metallic*.

**4.** **Adjudicative and Legislative Facts.** Professor Davis has argued that the appropriate distinction is that between adjudicative facts and legislative facts. Adjudicative facts are those surrounding the actors in an agency proceeding (what happened, who did it, when, where, why, and how). Legislative facts, in contrast, are the general facts to which the agency looks in deciding questions of law and policy. Adjudications generally focus on the former, while rulemaking focuses on the latter.

**5.** **Exceptions to *Londoner*.** In spite of the fact that the proceeding is adjudicatory in nature, a hearing will be required in cases of:

    a.    Mathematical rule or formula (where there is no agency discretion except the application of a reasonably precise standard to uncontroverted facts);

    b.    Inspections;

    c.    Tests; and

    d.    Elections.

Hollinrake
v. Law
Enforcement
Academy

**6.** **No Hearing Required When Decision Based on Legislative Facts--Hollinrake v. Law Enforcement Academy,** 452 N.W.2d 598 (Iowa 1990).

    a.    **Facts.** The Iowa Administrative Code allowed the Law Enforcement Academy (D) to certify as peace officers only applicants who have uncorrected vision of "not less than 20/100 in both eyes, corrected to 20/20." D interpreted the rule to require 20/20 corrected vision in each eye. Hollinrake (P) applied for certification, but did not have the required vision in his left eye, and D denied P certification without a hearing. P sought judicial review, but the district court dismissed his petition. P appeals.

**b.   Issue.** If a decision is based solely on legislative facts, does due process require a hearing?

**c.   Held.** No. Judgment affirmed.

1)   The law provides that when the granting of a license is required to be preceded by notice and an opportunity for an evidentiary hearing, the administrative hearing rules must be followed. But the law only provides for advance notice and hearing in the case of a revocation of an officer's certification, not for an application for certification.

2)   The law also provides that a hearing is required if an action involves the determination of disputed adjudicative facts, which are facts of particular applicability under the circumstances. But in this case, P does not contest the results of his eye examination, so there are no disputed adjudicative facts. P's deficiency does not involve circumstances peculiar to him, but instead involves a standardized vision requirement, which is a generalized legislative fact.

3)   The function of an evidentiary hearing is to find adjudicatory facts in the best way available. When there are no relevant adjudicative facts to dispute, there is no need for a hearing as a matter of due process.

**d.   Comment.** Adjudicative facts are the facts about the parties and their activities, businesses, and properties, involving questions of who did what, where, when, how, why, and with what motive or intent. Legislative facts do not relate to particular parties, but are generalized facts that apply more broadly and may serve as a ground for laying down a rule of law.

## C.   GENERAL VS. PARTICULAR RULES

1.   **General Rule.** Even when a single party is affected by agency rulemaking, the party may not be entitled to a formal hearing where the APA does not require it.

2.   **No Hearing Required for Rulemaking Proceeding--*In re* Appeal of Stratton Corp.,** 600 A.2d 297 (Vt. 1991).

*In re*
Appeal of
Stratton Corp.

**a.   Facts.** In response to a citizen petition, the Vermont Water Resources Board (D) initiated rulemaking proceedings to reclassify a brook. At the public hearing, Stratton Corp. (P), which owned property rights in the land adjoining the brook, claimed that due process required D to conduct formal, trial-like proceedings. D rejected P's argument and extended the public comment period to accommodate P. In its written materials, P pointed out that its land use permits would be subject to revocation or modification under the reclassification, and that it might be unable to obtain certain permits to develop its property. D adopted the reclassification rule anyway. P appealed to the superior court, which held for D. P appeals.

**b.** **Issue.** Where the legislature provides for a rulemaking proceeding, does due process require an adjudicative hearing if the action will have general applicability?

**c.** **Held.** No. Judgment affirmed.

1) The statute evinces a clear intent that the reclassification process be a rulemaking proceeding resulting in a rule. Due process requirements apply to administrative procedures only if they are adjudicative, and an adjudication is something that is based on the particular facts concerning specific parties.

2) There are three factors to determine whether an agency action is rulemaking or adjudication: (i) whether the inquiry is of a generalized nature instead of having an individualized focus; (ii) whether the inquiry focuses on a policy-type question instead of resolving factual disputes; and (iii) whether the result has prospective application and future effect.

3) In this case, the reclassification inquiry clearly involves generalized issues beyond the scope of the immediate parties, including how the classification affects the interests of all the state's citizens. D's rule has no direct force of its own; it merely determines the quality standards and leaves actual management to an executive agency.

4) D's determination does not resolve factual disputes; it involves a policy question about the quality level of a public waterway in the public interest. Finally, the reclassification decision does not address past conduct, but is a rule of prospective applicability.

5) Even though the reclassification rule might affect P's interests, general rules necessarily affect individuals. D's rule affects the public generally, and P cannot turn a public issue into a private contest.

**d.** **Comment.** Holmes has suggested that the principal means of differentiating quasi-legislative from quasi-adjudicative agency proceedings is the "time test." The former is prospective in nature and of future effect, whereas the latter is predicated upon preexisting facts. Dickinson has promoted the "applicability test," based on the notion that a quasi-legislative act is general in applicability, but an adjudication is particular in effect.

## D. PRIVILEGES

1. **General Rule.** No process is due when the property interest being de-nied by an administrative agency is deemed to constitute no more than a mere "privilege." In the past, the privilege concept was the dominant rule governing procedural due process.

2. **Licenses.** Professional licenses have been deemed to constitute a "right" that could not be denied without due process. Licenses of lesser distinc-tion (*e.g.,* liquor licenses) were deemed to constitute mere "privileges" that could be either revoked or amended by government at will.

   a. **Liquor license--Smith v. Liquor Control Commission,** 169 N.W.2d 803 (Iowa 1969).

   Smith v.
   Liquor Control
   Commission

   1) **Facts.** Smith (P), owner of a tavern, objected to the Liquor Control Commission's (D's) summary revocation of its beer license because P sold beer to a minor. The district court re-versed D's decision to revoke P's liquor license but upheld D's decision to revoke P's beer license. P appealed the beer license revocation.

   2) **Issue.** Does summary revocation of a beer license without a hearing violate the holder's constitutionally protected interest in due process of law?

   3) **Held.** No Judgment affirmed.

      a) A liquor or beer license is a privilege granted by the state and is in no sense a property right. Therefore, it can be revoked without notice and a hearing.

      b) When the licensee accepts the license, he takes it with whatever conditions the state chooses to impose, includ-ing a summary revocation limitation.

3. **Immigration.** An alien seeking admission to the United States has been deemed to have no more than a "privilege" of entry, not a "right" and entry may be restricted upon whatever grounds the government may choose to impose.

4. **Government Employment and Contracts.** These have been regarded as analogous to private agreements, where the contracting individual was held to have no "rights" beyond those conferred by the contract.

5. **Government Largess.** Welfare, too, was deemed to constitute no more than a "privilege" and not a "right."

6. **Conditional Limitations.** Privileges could not only be revoked at will, they could also be limited with such conditions as the government deemed desirable.

7. **Unconstitutional Limitations.** However, government could not deprive or limit privileges on unconstitutional ground (*e.g.,* religious or racial discrimination).

## E. ENTITLEMENTS

1. **Erosion of Privilege Concept.** The growth of government and its licensing and welfare functions led to the recognition that continuing to treat these government actions as mere privileges would lead to unjust results. Justice Frankfurter argued in 1951 that merely because the interest conferred is deemed to be a privilege does not warrant the conclusion that government may revoke it arbitrarily. Beginning in the 1960s, several federal courts began to view the privilege-right distinction as archaic and ill-conceived. Even though a person held no recognized "right," the courts held that government could not deprive an individual of a liberty or property interest without due process of law.

2. **Determining What Process Is Due--Goldberg v. Kelly,** 397 U.S. 254 (1970). *Look at what is a statutory entitlement.*

Goldberg
v. Kelly

*development
of statutory
entitlement*

   a. **Facts.** Kelly (P) was a recipient of public assistance payments in New York. P's benefits were terminated after an informal review by government officials but without giving P an opportunity for a hearing until after the termination. P challenged the procedure, claiming it deprived him of due process. The lower courts held that only a pretermination evidentiary hearing would satisfy the constitutional requirements. Goldberg (D), a government official, appeals.

   b. **Issue.** Must the government provide an opportunity for an evidentiary hearing before it terminates public assistance to a recipient?

   c. **Held.** Yes. Judgment affirmed.

      1) Welfare benefits are a statutory entitlement to those qualified to receive them. Termination of such benefits is state action. The extent of the process due to such recipients depends on the balance between the recipient's interest in avoiding the loss and the government's interest in summary adjudication.

*get away
from privilege
+ property
rights*

      2) By definition, a person entitled to receive welfare needs the assistance for essentials such as food, clothing, housing, and medical care. Termination of benefits, despite a controversy

over eligibility, may deprive an eligible recipient of the necessities of life. The same governmental interests behind the welfare program also support its continuation to eligible recipients. D would outweigh these interests by the need to conserve governmental fiscal and administrative resources, but the latter interests are not overriding in the welfare context. Thus, welfare benefits may not be terminated without due process.

3. **Citizen Initiative Cannot Take Away Private Property Rights--Brookpark Entertainment, Inc. v. Taft,** 951 F.2d 710 (6th Cir. 1991).

Brookpark
Entertainment,
Inc. v. Taft

   a. **Facts.** Brookpark Entertainment, Inc. (P) operated a nightclub that served liquor. The Ohio Department of Liquor Control suspended P's liquor license for several months, and later found that P had violated the suspension by selling liquor, but the Department took no further action. However, a group of citizens obtained enough signatures to put P's liquor license on a referendum ballot pursuant to a state "particular premises" local option law. P challenged the law prior to the election. Taft (D), the Ohio Secretary of State, moved for dismissal. The federal district court dismissed the suit, and P appeals.

   b. **Issue.** May a state give citizens the right, through the election process, to deprive an owner of property rights?

   c. **Held.** No. Judgment reversed.

      1) The Due Process Clause of the Fourteenth Amendment protects against the deprivation of life, liberty, and property without due process. D claims that P's liquor license is not property, but the term "property" has a broad definition for due process purposes.

      2) Ohio law provides that liquor licenses may be transferred, sold, inherited, and renewed, which shows that they have pecuniary value to their holders. A holder of an Ohio liquor license also has the right to a hearing before revocation and the right to appeal any adverse determination. These are more attributes of property than liquor licenses.

      3) The Ohio Supreme Court has held that a liquor licensee has no property interests because the legislature could terminate the license, but this holding is not binding because the label is not determinative. Besides, the fact that the state creates the license does not give the state the right to take it back without due process. "Property" cannot be defined by the procedures provided for its deprivation; the right to due process is conferred by constitutional guarantee, not by legislative grace.

4) Since P's liquor license is property, P cannot be deprived of the license without due process, which in this case means prior notice and a hearing. The referendum statute is therefore unconstitutional.

4. **Hearing for School Suspension--Goss v. Lopez,** 419 U.S. 565 (1975).

a. **Facts.** Lopez and other high school students (Ps) were suspended for 10 days by Goss (D), the school administrator, who had witnessed them disrupting a class and physically attacking a police officer. No hearing was given prior to suspension, but each student was given an opportunity to attend a post-suspension conference. The lower court found that the suspension process denied Ps due process. D appeals.

b. **Issue.** Must high school students ordinarily be given a hearing prior to disciplinary suspension?

c. **Held.** Yes. Judgment affirmed.

1) The Fifth and Fourteenth Amendments protect against the deprivation of life, liberty, and property without due process of law. Protected property interests are ordinarily not created by the Constitution, but are identified by independent sources such as statutes and rules entitling individuals to certain benefits.

2) Ohio created a legitimate claim of entitlement in public education, and this is a property interest protected by the Due Process Clause. Having conferred the interest, the state may not revoke it on grounds of misconduct without holding a hearing to determine whether misconduct has actually occurred.

3) An injury to reputation arising as a result of government action may also create due process obligations.

4) Before a student may be suspended for disciplinary reasons, he must be given oral or written notice of the charges against him, an explanation of the evidence, and an opportunity to rebut it. There need not be an opportunity for representation by counsel, to confront or cross-examine witnesses, or other ingredients of a formal hearing, at least for a relatively brief suspension such as 10 days.

5) A student whose presence poses a continuing danger to persons or property, or even an ongoing threat of disrupting the academic process, may be removed immediately, but then a hearing should follow as soon as possible.

d. **Dissent** (Powell, J., Burger, C.J., Blackmun, Rehnquist, JJ.). Intruding into the day-to-day operation of the public schools will create chaos in the educational system, and will likely open a floodgate of new litigation.

5. **Narrowing the Hearing Requirement--Mathews v. Eldridge,** 424 U.S. 319 (1976).

a. **Facts.** Eldridge (P) was awarded Social Security disability insurance benefits in 1968. About four years later, the state agency that administered the benefits determined, based on medical reports, that P's disability terminated. The agency so notified P by letter, and after receiving a written rebuttal from P, terminated P's benefits. Rather than seek reconsideration, P sued, seeking an immediate reinstatement of benefits pending a hearing on the issue of his disability. The lower courts, relying on *Goldberg*, upheld P's claim. Mathews (D) appeals.

b. **Issue.** Is a recipient of disability insurance benefits entitled to an evidentiary hearing prior to the initial termination of benefits?

c. **Held.** No. Judgment reversed.

   1) The requirements of due process vary depending on the particular circumstances involved. In setting forth the constitutional requirements, courts must balance the private interest affected, together with the risk of an erroneous deprivation and the added value of additional procedural safeguards, against the government's interest.

   2) P's sole interest is in continuing payments, because if on reconsideration he prevails, he will receive full retroactive relief. Unlike in *Goldberg*, a disabled person has other sources of income; disability payments are not based on financial need. Welfare benefits are available if the termination of disability places P below the subsistence level. Thus, P's interest is significant, but less than was at issue in *Goldberg*.

   3) The administrative pretermination procedures are less likely to err in disability cases as opposed to welfare cases because in the former, only medical records are involved. Welfare cases require consideration of a variety of factors. P was notified and given a chance to respond before benefits were terminated. An oral evidentiary hearing would add little.

   4) Finally, the government's interest in conserving resources must be considered, even though financial cost is not the controlling factor. Weight must be given to the good faith judgments of those who administer the disability programs.

Pg 407
The procedures
tailored to
ē needs
of those to
be heard.

6. **Hearing Requirements.** Based on *Goldberg v. Kelly*, *supra*, the courts have given increased attention to the actual procedural safeguards against invasion of private liberty and property rights. Once the existence of a constitutionally protected interest in life, liberty, or property is established, the courts must examine the adequacy of the procedures afforded. The courts must weigh the following factors to determine the extent of the procedures required: (i) the importance of the individual interest involved; (ii) the value of specific procedural safeguards to that interest; and (iii) the governmental interest in fiscal and administrative efficiency. A fair hearing need only have the following attributes:

a. Notice of the reasons for a proposed termination and a hearing at a meaningful time and in a meaningful manner;

b. The right to confront and cross-examine adverse witnesses;

c. The right to counsel, although the state need not furnish counsel in all cases;

d. A decision resting on the legal rules and evidence adduced at the hearing, shown by a statement of the reasons for the decision and the evidence relied on; and

e. An impartial decisionmaker.

## F. EXCEPTIONS TO THE HEARING PROCESS

Sandin v. Conner

1. **The Narrowing Scope of Liberty and Property Interests--Sandin v. Conner,** 515 U.S. 472 (1995).

    a. **Facts.** Conner (P) was serving a 30 years to life prison term in a Hawaiian prison. He was subjected to a strip and body cavity search, which he resisted. His resistance resulted in a hearing at which he was refused his request to present witnesses. P was sentenced to disciplinary segregation. He appealed, and a deputy administrator found the misconduct charge unsupported, and expunged P's disciplinary record. The court of appeals held that P had a liberty interest in being free of disciplinary segregation.

    b. **Issue.** Did state prison regulations create a liberty interest protected by the Due Process Clause?

    c. **Held.** No. Judgment reversed.

        1) Though several Supreme Court cases suggest that state regulations can create a liberty interest subject to due process protections, these decisions have had two undesirable effects: (i) they have created disincentives for states to codify prison manage-

ment procedures in the interest of enhancing uniformity of treatment; and (ii) they have involved the federal courts in the day-to-day management of prisons.

2) Though states may create liberty interests protected by the Due Process Clause, these interests will generally be limited to freedom from restraint that imposes atypical and significant hardship on the inmate in relation to the ordinary incidents of prison life.

3) Neither the Hawaiian prison regulation in question, nor the Due Process Clause, gave P a protected liberty interest that would authorize him more procedural protection than that conferred to him.

2. **Property Interests--Colson v. Sillman,** 35 F.3d 106 (2d Cir. 1994).

a. **Facts.** Colson and others (Ps) were physically handicapped minors who sought treatment and rehabilitation under state law. Ps claimed that the county and state had failed to provide timely written notice of the outcome of their applications, and an administrative appeals procedure. The district court held that Ps had a legitimate claim of entitlement in treatment and rehabilitation triggering procedural due process protection.

b. **Issue.** Do Ps have a legitimate claim of entitlement in treatment and rehabilitation?

c. **Held.** No. Judgment reversed and vacated.

1) To have a legally cognizable property interest in a government benefit, one must have more than a unilateral expectation of it; he must have a legitimate claim of entitlement.

2) The state statute at issue provides for treatment and rehabilitation only "within the limits of the appropriations made therefore." Since no sums were appropriated by the state legislature for the program, the program does not create a legitimate claim of entitlement. The program is discretionary within the judgment of state officials.

3. **Inadequate Pretermination Notice--Weston v. Hammonds,** Case No. 99CV412 (Denver District Court 1999).

a. **Facts.** Congress passed the Welfare Reform Act of 1996, which substituted the Temporary Assistance to Needy Families ("TANF") program for the Aid to Families with Dependent Children ("AFDC") program. To implement the legislation, the following year, Colorado created the Colorado Works Program, to be administered by the counties. Adams County adopted a process in which recipients whose benefits would be reduced would receive a computer-generated notice that contained no case-specific information. This class-action lawsuit was brought by aid recipients (Ps) to challenge these procedures.

  **b.**   **Issue.** Do these procedures satisfy due process requirements?

  **c.**   **Held.** No. Judgment for Ps.

   1)   Although both the federal and state statutes explicitly provide that cash assistance under the TANF program is not an entitlement, this court finds otherwise. The provisions of the statutes are mandatory. The legislature cannot constitutionally prevent due process rights from attaching.

   2)   In a case such as this, the plaintiff must prove (i) that a constitutionally cognizable interest is at stake, and if so, (ii) that the procedures employed were constitutionally deficient.

   3)   For a pretermination notice to be adequate it must be in writing and in terms comprehensible to the recipient, explaining precisely what the agency intends to do and its reasons for doing so, so that the recipient can assess the correctness of the agency's decision and make an informed decision as to whether to appeal. The notices here were inadequate as a matter of law.

## G.   MASS JUSTICE AND ADVERSARY PROCEDURE

  **1.**   **Administrative Efficiency.** Many have argued that the requirement of formal, trial-type proceedings may consume excessive agency resources of time and capital and may actually deprive the truly needy of economic assistance by depleting finite funds. Sometimes the requirements of such elaborate "due process" may exceed the savings realized by terminating benefits to an ineligible recipient.

  **2.**   **Alternative Proposals.** Some commentators and judges have recommended that an investigatory model would be preferable to the adversarial model. Having a neutral examiner review the evidence would still give the individual affected an opportunity for an oral hearing with counsel present, but would not require the agency to be represented. Social Security hearings are conducted this way.

## H.   WAIVER

Due process consists of notice and an opportunity to be heard. Like other constitutional guarantees, the hearing opportunity before administrative agencies can be, and in fact frequently is, waived.

1. **Opportunity for Hearing--National Independent Coal Operator's Association v. Kleppe,** 423 U.S. 388 (1976).

   a. **Facts.** The Secretary of the Interior (P) issued regulations pursuant to the Federal Coal Mine and Safety Act ("FCMSA") requiring union operators to timely protest and request adjudication of any penalties imposed upon them or else be deemed to have waived their protest and adjudication rights. FCMSA section 109(a)(3) provides that a "civil penalty shall be assessed by the Secretary only after the person charged with a violation . . . has been given an opportunity for a public hearing. . . ." Several mine operators (Ds) argued that under that section, no civil penalty could be enforced unless a formal hearing were held, even when no hearing had been requested. The court of appeals found for P. Ds appeal.

   b. **Issue.** May P assess a civil penalty without a hearing when the mine operator has failed to request one?

   c. **Held.** Yes. Judgment affirmed.

      1) The statute requires no more than an "opportunity" for a hearing. None was requested here, although the opportunity existed.

      2) P has a sufficient factual predicate to decide the case, absent a request for hearing: the reports of the inspectors who found the violations.

      3) In any event, where penalties are assessed, they may be reviewed on appeal by the district courts.

2. **Failure to Show Need.** Other decisions have upheld the agency's refusal to grant a hearing when the party requesting it failed to satisfy its burden of tendering sufficient evidence demonstrating a need for a hearing. This approach has also been endorsed by the Administrative Conference.

# I. POSTPONED HEARINGS

1. **General Rule.** Although agencies usually issue their decisions only after affording the parties "some kind of hearing," there appears to be no obligation to hold the hearing prior to an agency decision when only property rights are involved.

2. **Judicial Review.** Several cases have held that due process is satisfied if the hearing is that provided by judicial review of agency action, at least when such review consists of a trial de novo, offering the aggrieved party a full and complete opportunity to present his case on appeal.

National
Independent
Coal Operator's
Association
v. Kleppe

3. **Judicial Review Satisfies Due Process Requirements--Haskell v. Department of Agriculture,** 930 F.2d 816 (10th Cir. 1991).

   a. **Facts.** The Department of Agriculture (D) permanently disqualified Haskell (P) from participating in the food stamp program because his store had been charged with 13 violations of applicable regulations. P did not receive an evidentiary hearing at the administrative level, and sought de novo review of D's decision in federal district court. The district court granted D's motion for summary judgment. P appeals.

   b. **Issue.** If a party receives de novo review of an agency's administrative action in federal court, does it matter that he was deprived of due process by the agency?

   c. **Held.** No. Judgment affirmed.

      1) The district court determined that P had received adequate procedural due process during D's administrative hearings. Even if this finding was erroneous, he did receive judicial review de novo.

      2) This review renders irrelevant the question of whether the administrative process provided due process.

J. **EMERGENCY CASES**

   1. **General Rule.** Where unusual circumstances exist, courts have upheld the deprivation of property with a hearing postponed until after the government acts. Three criteria have been identified where post-hearing seizure of property has been upheld.

      a. **Important public interest.** The seizure must be necessary to satisfy an important governmental interest. For example, prehearing seizures of mislabeled consumer products or dangerous materials have been upheld, and serious financial risks to the public or the government can justify seizures.

      b. **Promptness.** There must be a significant urgency for prompt action; *i.e.,* the emergency must be actual.

      c. **Control.** The government official responsible for determining the need for the seizure must be the one initiating it.

   2. **National Bank Regulation--FDIC v. Mallen,** 486 U.S. 230 (1988).

      a. **Facts.** Mallen (P) was president and a director of a federally insured bank supervised by the FDIC (D). P was indicted for making false statements to D, and pursuant to its statutory authority, D suspended P from his positions with the bank and prohibited him from further participation in managing the bank. P sought a preliminary injunction. The district court declared the suspension null and void and enjoined D from enforcing it on the ground that D failed to give P a hearing before taking action. D appeals.

b.   **Issue.** May an agency deprive a party of property without due process to respond to an emergency if authorized by statute and if it provides a post-deprivation hearing?

c.   **Held.** Yes. Judgment reversed.

   1)   P's interest in continued employment and his ownership in the bank constitute property interests protected by the Due Process Clause. D deprived P of these interests by suspending P. The only issue is what process is due.

   2)   P admits that an important government interest, accompanied by a substantial assurance that the deprivation is not baseless, may in limited cases demanding prompt action justify postponing the opportunity to be heard until after the initial deprivation. P's indictment was sufficient to arrest him, and is sufficient as well to justify the suspension without a hearing.

   3)   P claims D's post-deprivation proceedings are not prompt enough. The statute requires D to hold a hearing within 30 days and then notify P of its decision within 60 days of the hearing, which gives D a total of 90 days to hear the case and reach its decision. This is not excessive, because there is a strong public interest in a full evaluation of the evidence.

   4)   The statute does not guarantee an opportunity to present oral testimony, but leaves it to D's discretion. But oral testimony is not always essential, and in this case, P made no offer of proof to justify review.

## K.   FLEXIBLE DUE PROCESS

1.   **Ambiguous Standards.** The United States Supreme Court has few concrete standards to govern the question of what process is "due." The lower courts have been left to struggle with the constitutional question on an ad hoc basis, depending on the factual circumstances present in each individual case. This flexible due process approach requires a balancing approach, weighing the competing governmental and private interests involved. Some courts engage in a cost-benefit analysis.

**2.** **Type of Notice and Hearing Required by Due Process--Gray Panthers v. Schweiker,** 716 F.2d 23 (D.C. Cir. 1983).

a. **Facts.** The Gray Panthers and three named Medicaid beneficiaries (Ps) brought suit to challenge procedures adopted by Schweiker (D), the Secretary of Health, Education, and Welfare, for resolving disputes concerning claims for less than $100. Medicare is principally administered through insurance companies under contract with the government. Individuals submitting claims for payment or reimbursement for sums of less than $100 are not entitled to a hearing, although those filing claims exceeding $100 are given one. Ps challenged these procedures on due process grounds. D argued that the cost of additional procedures for such small claims outweighed the benefits of oral hearings. The district court found for D. Ps appeal.

b. **Issue.** Are informal oral hearings required in every case of claims for Medicare benefits?

c. **Held.** No.

1) A flexible approach that considers the interrelationship between notice and hearing requirements is desirable.

2) For the majority of Medicare claims involving less than $100, a combination of a toll-free "telephone hearing" and a full written hearing for cases involving only mathematical errors or improper documentation is sufficient to satisfy the minimum requirements of due process.

3) Informal oral, face-to-face hearings are required only in cases involving credibility or veracity (if such cases are sufficient in number to justify different treatment).

# VI. EVIDENTIARY HEARINGS AND DECISIONS

## A. INTRODUCTION

Assuming that there is a right to a trial-type formal hearing, what are the procedural obligations of the agency?

## B. PARTIES IN INTEREST AND INTERVENTION

1. **Standing to Intervene.** Modern courts have allowed a wide spectrum of interest groups the right to be represented before administrative agencies, including groups suffering technological interference, economic injury, consumer injury, and aesthetic or ecological injury. The issue of standing to intervene is related to the question of standing to appeal adverse agency action. In either case, one who suffers an adverse effect is ordinarily deemed to have standing.

2. **Consumer Groups--Office of Communication v. FCC,** 359 F.2d 994 (D.C. Cir. 1966).

   Office of Communication v. FCC

   a. **Facts.** The FCC granted an applicant's renewal of its television license, denying the petition from the Office of Communication (P), a consumer group, seeking to intervene to oppose the application on grounds of racist programming and excessive commercials.

   b. **Issue.** Do consumers have standing before an administrative agency to intervene in pending proceedings?

   c. **Held.** Yes.

      1) Prior cases allowed standing to those who suffered electronic interference or economic injury.

      2) Standing is a practical and functional concept designed to limit agency participation only to those with a legitimate interest. Certainly the viewing audience has an acute interest in television programming. Consumers are excellent vindicators of the public interest.

      3) Although the agency need not allow all potential intervenors to participate, it must allow some audience participation in license renewal proceedings. The agency should be allowed broad discretion to promulgate rules defining criteria governing who may participate, consonant with its needs for administrative economy and efficiency.

3. **Consolidation of Mutually Exclusive Applications.** Since the landmark decision of *Ashbacker Radio Corp. v. FCC*, 318 U.S. 327 (1945), admin-

istrative agencies have not been free to grant one application without some consideration of a timely filed separate application for the same franchise. Thus, if only one license is likely to be issued, it is incumbent on the agency to hold a comparative hearing.

**Sarasota County Public Hospital v. Department of Health**

4.  **Comparative Review Required--Sarasota County Public Hospital v. Department of Health,** 553 So. 2d 189 (Fla. Dist. App. Ct. 1989).

    a.  **Facts.** The Sarasota County Public Hospital (P) filed a certificate of need application with the Department of Health (D) to build an acute care hospital. Another hospital, Doctors Hospital, filed a similar application at the same time. D did not compare the two applications, but notified P that its application would be denied while Doctors' would be approved. P petitioned for a comparative review, but D dismissed P's petition, noting that P's proposal would duplicate Doctors'. P appeals the dismissal.

    b.  **Issue.** Must an agency considering two applications that are mutually exclusive provide comparative review before making a decision?

    **Held.** Yes. Judgment reversed.

    1)  The Supreme Court held in *Ashbacker Radio Corp. v. FCC*, 318 U.S. 327 (1945), that the grant of one of two bona fide and mutually exclusive applications for administrative approval without a hearing on both deprives the loser of the hearing to which it is entitled. This principle is not based on any statutory provision but on the fundamental doctrine of fair play.

    2)  The fundamental doctrine of fair play applies in this case because D did consider Doctors' application when it reviewed P's. P must have an opportunity to be heard at the same time as Doctors instead of after Doctors.

## C. NOTICE AND PLEADINGS

1.  **Notice.** Notice is a fundamental component of due process. Notice must be timely given and contain sufficient information to allow the individual a reasonable opportunity to prepare her case. The APA requires that notice apprise the affected party of the "matters of fact and law asserted." [APA §554(a)] Hence, it must not only advise her of the date and place of hearing, it must also inform her of the substantive issues to be addressed. Defects in notice may be cured with evidence that the individual actually knew the substance of the matters that would be adjudicated. Agency notice may be served by registered mail.

> "In fixing ē time & place for hearings, due regard shall be had for ē convenience of ē pty / rep."
>
> ⇓
>
> a ct can intervene if arbitrariness is shown in ē agency's fixing of ē hearing place.
> E.g. hearing for a Guam resident (disability claim) in Hawaii

2. **Issuance of Complaint Not Subject to Judicial Review.** The issuance of a complaint alleging unlawful conduct is not a final agency action, and hence, not subject to judicial review.

3. **Curing Defective Notice.** Even though an agency's initial notice may fail to specify all the issues to be adjudicated, if the individual is subsequently given actual notice of additional issues and an opportunity to present evidence in response thereto, she cannot successfully challenge the notice as deficient, unless she was prejudiced either by delay or by informality in the subsequent actual notice.

4. **Agency Cannot Change Theory of Case During Adjudication Without Notice--Yellow Freight System v. Martin,** 954 F.2d 353 (6th Cir. 1992).

Yellow Freight System v. Martin

   a.  **Facts.** Moyer, an employee of the Yellow Freight System (P), aggravated a preexisting medical condition while descending from his truck to see what was wrong with the truck. Moyer abandoned the truck and was taken to the hospital, and as a result did not follow P's procedures for mechanical breakdowns. P suspended Moyer. After Moyer testified for Lee, a fellow employee who had filed a grievance against P, P fired him. Moyer filed a complaint with Martin (D), the Secretary of Labor, claiming P violated federal law (section 405(b) of the Surface Transportation Assistance Act) by discharging him in retaliation for refusing to drive a truck when he was ill. D's regional administrator investigated and determined that Moyer's complaint had no merit. Moyer requested an administrative hearing, and based on the ALJ's recommendations, D concluded that P had not violated section 405(b). However, D did conclude that P violated section 405(a) by retaliating against Moyer for his testimony against P at Lee's grievance hearing. D ordered P to reinstate Moyer. P sued, claiming a violation of due process and seeking a review of D's decision.

   *[handwritten margin note: DP is not offended if an agency decides an issue & pty F & F litigated @ trial. When pty fully litigate an issue, they obviously have notice of e issue & have been given an opp to respond]*

   b.  **Issue.** When an agency conducts a hearing based on one set of allegations, may it *[handwritten: may not]* render a decision based on a separate but related set of facts?

   c.  **Held.** No. Judgment reversed.

      1)  Procedural due process requires notice and an opportunity to be heard. Section 554(b) of the APA provides that parties entitled to notice of any agency hearing shall be timely informed of the matters of fact and law asserted. This means that an agency must give the party charged a clear statement of the theory on which the agency will proceed with the case. An agency cannot change theories without providing reasonable notice, and especially cannot raise a related charge after the hearing record is closed.

2) In this case, D did not notify P about the section 405(a) issue. D's letter notifying P of Moyer's complaint referred only to the section 405(b) issue, and no notice was ever given to D prior to the administrative hearing.

3) D claims that P impliedly consented to litigate the section 405(a) issue by introducing evidence at the hearing that showed P discharged Moyer for testifying at Lee's grievance proceeding. During a hearing, parties may by implied or express consent raise issues not formally raised in the pleadings, and the court may treat these issues as if they had been raised in the pleadings. However, the record does not support D's contention that P did or should have understood that the evidence raised a section 405(a) issue. Therefore, D failed to give P prior notice of the issue, and P did not have an opportunity to respond before D found a violation of section 405(a).

## D. NATURE OF HEARING

1. **Formal Adjudication.** Formal agency adjudication closely resembles a trial-type hearing before a judge sitting without a jury.

2. **Public Hearing.** Ordinarily, due process requires a public hearing if formal adjudication is mandated. However, a private hearing may be offered if necessary to protect the interests of the affected individual.

3. **Hearing on Whether to Close a Hearing--Johnson Newspaper Corp. v. Melino,** 564 N.E.2d 1046 (N.Y. 1990).

   a. **Facts.** Johnson Newspaper Corp. (P) sought access to a disciplinary hearing involving a dentist who was a licensed professional supervised by the Board of Regents under state law. The law provided for an adversarial hearing on charges of misconduct. The hearing panel would then prepare a written report with recommendations, the Board's review committee would review the report and hearing transcript and make its own report, and then the full Board would review both reports and make a final decision. The Board refused P's request on grounds that its policy kept professional disciplinary hearings closed unless the accused requested an open proceeding. P sued for access, but the lower courts dismissed the suit. P appeals.

   b. **Issue.** Is there a public right of access to professional disciplinary hearings conducted pursuant to state law?

   c. **Held.** No. Judgment affirmed.

      1) P claims a constitutional right of public access. The Supreme Court set forth a two-tiered test that involves consideration first of whether the place and process have historically been open

*[handwritten margin notes:]*

*Johnson Newspaper Corp. v. Melino*

*Generally, the hearing is presumed to be open & may not be closed to public unless a compelling reason is demonstrated & affected members are given an opp. to be heard.*

*Dr can waive a right but ē media can't*

to the press and general public, followed by consideration of whether public access plays a significant positive role in the functioning of the particular process in question.

2) Applying this test, the Supreme Court has held that the public has a right of access to voir dire proceedings and preliminary hearings in criminal cases. But there is no tradition of professional disciplinary hearings being open to the public. Nor is there any evidence that public access plays a significant positive role in such proceedings.

3) P also claims a common law right. While there is a strong public policy favoring public access to judicial and administrative proceedings, in this case the statute contains a policy of preserving the confidentiality of information pertaining to disciplinary proceedings until a determination is reached. The Board itself has an established policy of privacy. This policy protects potential complainants who might otherwise be deterred from disclosing confidential or private information to make a complaint, and it also reflects concern about the effect on a professional's reputation resulting from unfounded accusations.

## E.   COUNSEL

1. **Right to Representation by Counsel.** An individual is ordinarily entitled to the opportunity to retain an attorney. [APA §555(b)] However, this general rule does not entitle a party in an agency proceeding to counsel provided at public expense.

   *qualified rep.*
   represented by someone other than an attorney is permissible

2. **Statutory Prohibition.** Statutes that prohibit the presence of counsel in certain contexts have survived constitutional challenge.

3. **Statutory Limitation on Attorneys' Fees--Department of Labor v. Triplett,** 494 U.S. 715 (1990).

   Department of Labor v. Triplett

   a. **Facts.** The Black Lung Benefits Act, administered by the Department of Labor (P), provides for compensation to miners disabled by specified diseases. Benefits are awarded after adjudication and, if requested, review by an ALJ, the Benefits Review Board, and a Federal Court of Appeals. Claimants may be represented by counsel, who may receive a "reasonable attorney's fee" from the trust fund if the claimant wins a contested case. However, an attorney may not receive any fee, including from the claimant, unless approved by the appropriate agency or court, and P's regulations invalidate all contracts for fees. Triplett (D), an attorney, received unapproved fees by taking cases on a 25% contingency basis. The West Virginia State Bar held a hearing and recommended a suspension, but the state supreme court denied enforcement on the ground that the constraints on attorneys' fees effectively denied claimants "the procedural safeguards provided by Congress that are essential to vindicate the right to benefits also granted by Congress." The Supreme Court granted certiorari.

**b.** **Issue.** May a federal law prohibit the acceptance of attorneys' fees for the representation of claimants before an administrative agency, except fees approved by the agency?

**c.** **Held.** Yes. Judgment reversed.

1) Congress created the fee limitation scheme and there is a strong presumption of constitutionality for carefully considered decisions of a coequal and representative branch of the government. The fee limitation pursues the legitimate interest of protecting claimants from their improvident contracts, which benefits themselves, their families, and the public.

*[handwritten note: 1) claimant could not obtain rep  2) b/c of ē regulation (causation)]*

) In *Walters v. National Association of Radiation Survivors*, 473 U.S. 305 (1985), the Court upheld a fee limitation scheme that would make attorneys unavailable to claimants because attorneys were not essential to vindicate the claims. In this case, D has not even shown that P's scheme will make attorneys unavailable. D merely produced some anecdotal evidence about what three different lawyers believed about the impact of the scheme.

*[handwritten note: No right to ct appointed counsel in admin. agency hearing (N 3 pp. 496)*

*No right to counsel for prisoners (Wolff vs. McDonnell)]*

Even if D had shown that attorneys were unavailable, he did not show that its cause was the regulation of fees. Contingent-fee arrangements are common, and the fact that D would not receive a fee unless he won the case is basically like the contingent fee scenario.

**4.** **Investigatory Proceedings.** There is no right to representation by an attorney in investigatory proceedings that are noncriminal in nature.

**5.** **Representation by Nonattorneys.** Although licensed attorneys are free to practice before almost all federal agencies, administrative practice is not limited to lawyers. Several agencies allow non-lawyer practitioners to appear before them. For example, the Interstate Commerce Commission administers an examination, the successful completion of which allows nonlawyer transportation practitioners to practice before the agency.

## F. FROM EXAMINERS TO ADMINISTRATIVE LAW JUDGES

**1.** **The One Who Decides Must Hear.** In its seminal decision of *Morgan v. United States*, 298 U.S. 468 (1936), the United States Supreme Court held that, in administrative adjudications, "the one who decides must actually hear." This statement is not to be taken literally, however, as the court meant that the decisionmaker need merely carefully consider the evidence and the positions of the parties. He may delegate to subordinates the tasks of conducting the oral adjudication, taking the evidence, and subsequently sifting and analyzing it. The decisionmaker need not actually hear and observe the witnesses. But he must consider the evidence and render a decision based thereon.

2. **Agency's Decision Based on Evidence It Did Not Hear--Guerrero v. New Jersey,** 643 F.2d 148 (3d Cir. 1981).

Guerrero v.
New Jersey

    a.   **Facts.** Dr. Guerrero (P) was found guilty of medical malpractice by the New Jersey Board of Medical Examiners (D). The Board did not actually hear the evidence, but delegated the task of conducting the oral adjudication to an administrative law judge ("ALJ"). P filed suit, claiming that he was denied due process because D itself did not hear the testimony. The district court upheld D's decision. P appeals.

    b.   **Issue.** May a decisional body render a decision on the basis of evidence it has not actually heard?

    c.   **Held.** Yes. Judgment affirmed.

        1)   D's procedures for the taking of evidence by an [...] ther the Due Process nor the Equal Protection Cla[...] States Constitution. Neither requires that the indi[...] and observed the witnesses render the ultimate [...]

        2)   The ALJ here heard the evidence and filed a writ[...] D. P had an opportunity to file exceptions to t[...] mended decision before the ultimate decision w[...]

3. **Delegation.** The volume of agency business makes it vir[...] for heads of large agencies to preside at hearings. Hence, [...] rule rather than the exception.

4. **Hearing Examiners.** Agency examiners were made partially autonomous of agency political supervision and control with the promulgation of the APA in 1946.

5. **Administrative Law Judges.** The Civil Service Commission changed the title of hearing examiners to ALJs in 1972. Congress codified the effort with APA amendments in 1978. This change of nomenclature purportedly elevated the stature of these individuals. Today, ALJs are more numerous than federal judges.

*[handwritten notes:]*
ALJ
1) Trial examiners hear c̄ evidence.
2) Examiner made a report to c̄ agency
3) Parties response to c̄ report
4) Agency makes final decision
    N4 pp. 500

→ see c̄ notes pg

No contempt power

central panel, of ALJ rejected in c̄ fed level

*Legal Bias = Bias that requires an adjudicator to disqualify himself.*
*↑ applies equally in cts & agencies.*

## G. BIAS   *Contrast w/ rule making = cinderella rule: bias not applicable in rule makin[g]*

1. **General Rule.** A biased decisionmaker is inconsistent with fundamental notions of procedural due process.

   *Financial*

   a. **Pecuniary interest.** Anyone with a financial stake in the outcome of the proceeding is deemed biased. *most obvious type*

   b. **Personal prejudice.** One who has made up his mind about the particular facts involved or the culpability of the individual accused is impermissibly biased. The potential for this type of bias is greater in administrative procedures than it is in courts, because administrators typically deal with one type of case and may be prone to having a disposition to view all the cases as the same. Or they may have taken public positions on issues their agency deals with.

   c. **Difficulty of proof.** It is difficult to sustain a charge of prejudgment. Although the decisionmaker may have handled several similar proceedings involving the charged individual or other persons, and ruled against them all, it still must be demonstrated that the decisionmaker is incapable of judging a controversy fairly on the basis of its unique circumstances.

Gibson v.
Berryhill

*disqualification applies to admin. adjudicators too.*

2. **Indirect Financial Interest--Gibson v. Berryhill,** 411 U.S. 564 (1973).

   a. **Facts.** Employees of Lee Optical Co. (Ps) were charged with engaging in unprofessional conduct by the Alabama Board of Optometry (D) because Ps worked for a corporation that recent statutory changes had potentially made illegal. D consisted of only optometrists not employed by corporations. Ps challenged the fairness of D's hearing the case because if D concluded that Ps' operations were unlawful, D's members would presumably get Ps' business. The district court held for Ps. D appeals.

   b. **Issue.** May members of a state board who could benefit personally by the outcome of a case conduct hearings and make decisions on the matter?

   c. **Held.** No. Judgment affirmed.

      1) A pecuniary stake in the dispute by the decisionmaker need not be a direct one to disqualify the decisionmaker.

      2) The board was composed of individuals who would likely benefit from the license revocation of their competitors. This indirect financial gain arising from putting one's competitors out of business is deemed sufficient to warrant disqualification.

*Those w/ substantial pecuniary financial interest in ē proceedin[g] should not adjudicate these disputes.*

3. **Disqualifying Public Statements by Agency Official--1616 Second Ave. v. State Liquor Authority,** 550 N.E.2d 910 (N.Y. 1990).

a. **Facts.** 1616 Second Ave. (P) operated a restaurant with a liquor license. P attracted public attention when one of its patrons murdered another patron shortly after they left P's restaurant. P was charged by the State Liquor Authority (D) with selling alcoholic beverages to underage patrons. A state senate hearing called D's chairman, Duffy, to testify about D's operations. Among other things, Duffy discussed the charges against P, saying he was going to bring P "to justice" and that he wanted to make a record in P's case. D's charges were heard by an ALJ, who found P guilty. P contested the results, and the matter was referred to D's five commissioners, including Duffy. P requested that Duffy recuse himself, but he declined. With Duffy's participation, D imposed a suspension and fine on P. P sued to have the decision annulled. The lower courts upheld D. P appeals.

b. **Issue.** May an agency official's public statements regarding the merits of a pending case disqualify the official from participating in an administrative review of the case?

c. **Held.** Yes. Judgment reversed.

1) An impartial decisionmaker is a basic guarantee of due process and applies to adjudicatory proceedings before administrative agencies. Lack of impartiality includes such concepts as prior knowledge of facts, personal interest, animosity, favoritism, and prejudgment, but the application of any of these in a particular case depends on the specific facts.

2) Disqualification is more likely to be necessary when the official has a preconceived view of the facts in a specific case, as opposed to a view regarding general questions of law or policy. Administrative officials normally have specific and advanced knowledge regarding conditions in the area they regulate, so familiarity with the facts of a specific case or a public position on a policy issue does not require disqualification. It is when the official has a prejudgment of specific facts at issue in an adjudicatory proceeding that disqualification becomes necessary.

3) Duffy's testimony at the legislative hearing demonstrated his belief that P was guilty, and that the only issue was whether D could prove it because some of the witnesses lived out of state. Even if Duffy in fact had not actually prejudged the matter, his statements suggested that he had, and the appearance gave an impermissible air of unfairness to the proceeding.

*he will be disqualified on ground of prejdgmt if a disinterested observer may conclude that he has in some measure adjudged $\bar{c}$ facts & $\bar{c}$ law of a particular case in advance of hearing it*

*public stmt not ok*

*mere familarity w/ facts or holding a public posi on on a policy issue*

*ok & (PP 514)*

4) On remand, D should reconsider the findings without Duffy's participation.

**4. Fundamental Unfairness of Hearing--Rosa v. Bowen,** 677 F. Supp. 782 (D.N.J. 1988).

Rosa v. Bowen

*it is ē duty of an ALJ to develop an admin record fully + fairly, even where a claimant is represented by counsel.*

a. **Facts.** Rosa (P) applied for Social Security benefits. Bowen (D), Secretary of Health and Human Services, denied her application. The case was remanded by federal court for further administrative action, and ended up with an ALJ for a hearing. P was represented by an attorney at the hearing, but the ALJ was impatient, indifferent, and condescending throughout the proceeding. The hearing transcript reflected that the ALJ was in a hurry because he had a lot of cases and he wanted to go to lunch. He gave P advice about her health, compared her condition with his own mother's, and began bargaining to award P benefits in return for a change in the starting time of the benefits. The ALJ finally found that P was not disabled and issued a recommended decision to that effect. D adopted the ALJ's findings. P appeals to federal court.

b. **Issue.** May a court invalidate the results of an administrative hearing if it concludes that the ALJ failed to provide a completely fair hearing?

c. **Held.** Yes. Judgment reversed.

1) Normally, a court reviewing D's decisions simply determines whether there is substantial evidence to support the decisions. A court may also, however, determine whether the claimant received a fair and impartial hearing.

2) If a court finds that the hearing was not fair, it may remand the case to D for further hearings. In this case, D provided a hearing that was not fair because of the attitude and conduct of the ALJ. Excessive concern with expedience, indifference, and the rest can undermine the fairness of a proceeding. While no single error of the ALJ's would probably have forced a remand, the cumulative effect rendered the hearing unfair.

**H. RULE OF NECESSITY**

Courts are frequently reluctant to hold a particular tribunal disqualified for bias where there exists no alternative forum to adjudicate the controversy.

**I. COMBINATION OF FUNCTIONS**

1. **Administrative Procedure Act.** The APA prohibits agency prosecutors or investigators from either deciding the case or advising the decisionmaker ex parte. [APA §554(d)]

a. **Formal adjudication.** The APA prohibition against commingling of functions literally pertains only to formal adjudications. Rulemaking or informal adjudication is implicitly exempt from the prohibition against commingling of functions.

b. **Agency heads.** The most important exception to APA section 554(d) is to agency heads, who are generally free to investigate, prosecute, and decide the controversy.

c. **Rulemaking.** Rulemaking is exempt from prohibition against commingling.

d. **Initial licensing.** Also exempt is initial licensing by an agency.

e. **Statutory exemptions.** Congress has, in legislation other than the APA, separately allowed commingling in other contexts, such as deportation hearings.

2. **Agency Heads Exempted--Withrow v. Larkin,** 421 U.S. 35 (1975).

Withrow → agency's
v. Larkin    role

a. **Facts.** Dr. Larkin (P) performed abortions at his office in Milwaukee. The Wisconsin Medical Board (D) instituted proceedings for the suspension of P's license. P sought an injunction against D on the ground that the commingling of investigatory and decisionmaking responsibilities deprived him of due process. The district court issued a preliminary injunction against D. D appeals.

b. **Issue.** Does the combination of investigation and decisionmaking functions destroy the impartiality of D so as to violate fundamental notions of due process?

c. **Held.** No. Judgment reversed and case remanded.

   1) Those claiming that the combination of investigative and adjudicatory functions creates impermissible bias must overcome a presumption of honesty and integrity of decisionmakers.

   2) Even the APA exempts agency heads *or members of ā body* from its prohibition against commingling.

   3) Judges frequently participate in the investigation or prosecution of proceedings prior to adjudication, and no claim is made that these activities violate due process.

3. **Former Counsel Cannot Participate in Adjudication--Beer Garden v. State Liquor Authority,** 590 N.E.2d 1193 (N.Y. 1992).

Beer Garden
v. State Liquor
Authority
↓
ind. participation

a. **Facts.** The State Liquor Authority (D) issued three formal notifications to Beer Garden (P) regarding D's intent to start proceedings to cancel or revoke P's liquor license. Each notice was issued over the stamped signature of "Sharon L. Tillman, counsel to the Authority." An ALJ conducted hearings on the revocation and suspension proceedings and found the allegations to be true. He referred the matter to D for final determination. Subsequently, Tillman became one of the five commissioners of D. Three of the five commissioners, including Tillman, then voted to adopt the ALJ's findings and revoke P's license. P requested a reconsideration and asked that Tillman recuse herself. She refused, and the original decision was sustained. P then sued.

b. **Issue.** When a commission adjudicates a license suspension proceeding, may a commissioner who was counsel to the commission when the charges were filed participate in the adjudication?

c. **Held.** No. Judgment reversed.

1) State law provides that no judge may sit in, or take any part in the decision of, an action, claim, matter, motion, or proceeding to which she is a party or in which she has been attorney or counsel. Although this law specifically applies only to courts, it represents the common law rule of disqualification that applies to administrative tribunals exercising quasi-judicial functions.

2) D claims that Tillman did not have actual knowledge of the facts, because her signature was merely stamped on the notices P received. Even if Tillman could act impartially in this case, it is a matter of propriety for administrative officers to recuse themselves if prior involvement creates an appearance of partiality. Her role as "prosecutor" in this case is inherently incompatible with her subsequent participation as a "judge" in the case.

d. **Comment.** The court noted that the judgment process must avoid any suspicion of the fairness and integrity of the judge. A judge disqualified under the statute may not act in a case even with the consent of the parties, because the law protects the interests of the general public as well as the parties in the specific case.

## J. EVIDENCE

1. **Liberal Rules.** The technical rules of evidence that apply in courts of law, including the hearsay rule, are largely relaxed in administrative proceedings.

2. **Legal Residuum.** Under the rule of *Carroll v. Knickerbocker Ice Co.*, 218 N.Y. 435 (1916), agency findings are insufficient unless supported by a residuum of evidence beyond mere hearsay.

3. **Legal Residuum Rule--Wagstaff v. Department of Employment Security,** 826 P.2d 1069 (Utah Ct. App. 1992).

a. **Facts.** Wagstaff (P) worked at Hill Air Force Base with a "secret" security clearance. During an investigation of drug use among civilian personnel at the base, several of P's coworkers implicated P as having used illegal drugs. When he was questioned, P admitted having used drugs on one occasion only. The Air Force terminated P for the drug use. P applied for unemployment benefits through the Department of Employment Security (D). D denied P's claim on the ground that P had been terminated for just cause. P requested a formal hearing. At the hearing, P repeated that his drug use was a one-time incident. The Air Force introduced the investigative report that contained hearsay testimony about additional drug use by P. The ALJ found that the Air Force did not show "just cause" and reversed D's initial decision. The Industrial Commission's Board of Review reversed the ALJ. P appeals.

b. **Issue.** May findings in an administrative hearing be based exclusively on hearsay evidence?

c. **Held.** No. Judgment reversed.

1) Hearsay evidence is admissible in administrative proceedings, and it was not improper for D to consider the evidence in the report. However, findings of fact may not be based exclusively on hearsay evidence. Findings must be supported by a residuum of legal evidence that would be competent in a court of law.

2) The only competent evidence in this case was P's own admission of one use and his denial of any other incidents. D's findings that P was involved in more than one instance must have been based on the report; there was no residuum of competent legal evidence to support the finding.

4. **Reliance on Written Reports Over Live Testimony--Richardson v. Perales,** 402 U.S. 389 (1971).

a. **Facts.** Perales (P) claimed that he became disabled while lifting an object at work, and filed a claim for Social Security disability insurance with the Department of Health, Education, and Welfare (D). D had several doctors review P's condition and sought to introduce their reports at D's disability hearing. The reports were allowed and P was denied disability benefits. The appellate court held that although the hearsay evidence was admissible, it did not amount to substantial evidence because it was controverted by live testimony. D appeals.

*Wagstaff v. Department of Employment Security*

*[handwritten margin note:] Hearsay is admissable*

*[handwritten margin note:] Can't make substantive finding based on hearsay alone. must be a residuum of other legal evidence*

*[handwritten margin note:] It is sufficient if it lends any support by way of corroboration even though through wholly circumstantial evidence.*

*Richardson v. Perales*

b. **Issue.** Do written reports of medical examiners constitute substantial evidence to support a finding of nondisability even when contradicted by evidence from live witnesses?

c. **Held.** Yes. Judgment reversed.

1) Substantial evidence is more than a mere scintilla. It means such relevant evidence as a reasonable mind might accept as adequate to support a conclusion.

2) The administrative burden on agencies such as the Social Security Administration is severe. The cost of providing live medical testimony in each of the several thousand proceedings would significantly deplete the resources required to satisfy the needs of the truly needy.

3) Truthfulness and veracity are not at issue here. The doctors' conclusions can adequately be assessed on the basis of the written record.

4) P did not exercise his right to subpoena the doctors and thereby avail himself of the opportunity to cross-examine them. Had P genuinely wanted to challenge their testimony, he should have insisted on the presence of the doctors at the hearing.

## K. BURDEN OF PROOF

1. **Burden of Proof.** The APA states that unless a statute provides to the contrary, the "proponent of a rule or order has the burden of proof." [5 U.S.C. §556(d)] *unless otherwise stated, ē standard is preponderance of ē evidence standard.*

2. **Substantial Evidence Rule.** The APA also provides that, in a proceeding subject to the requirements of formal adjudication, no decision may be issued unless "supported by and in accordance with reliable, probative and substantial evidence." [5 U.S.C. §556(d)]

Director, Office of Workers' Compensation Programs v. Greenwich Collieries

3. **True Doubt Rule--Director, Office of Workers' Compensation Programs v. Greenwich Collieries,** 512 U.S. 267 (1994).

a. **Facts.** Santoro's widow filed a claim for benefits under the Workers' Compensation Act against Mahler Terminals, Inc. After a hearing on the issue of whether the injury was work related, the Department of Labor's ("DOL") ALJ found the evidence evenly balanced, and applied the "true doubt" rule, under which the burden of persuasion is shifted to the party opposing the benefits claim. The court of appeals held that the "true doubt" rule was inconsistent with the DOL's regulations under the Black Lung Benefits Act, and the United States

Supreme Court's decision in *Mullins Coal Co. of Virginia v. Director, Office of Workers' Compensation Programs*, 484 U.S. 135 (1987). The Supreme Court granted certiorari.

**b.** **Issue.** Is the "true doubt" rule consistent with the APA, which provides that "except as otherwise provided by statute, the proponent of a rule or order has the burden of proof"?

**c.** **Held.** No. Judgment affirmed.

1) Exemptions to the APA are not lightly presumed. The ambiguous regulation in question does not overcome that these procedures are subject to the APA's burden of proof provision.

2) The term "burden of proof" is nowhere defined in the APA. Supreme Court decisions define the term as essentially synonymous with the "burden of persuasion." The burden of proof is the obligation that rests on one of the parties to persuade the trier of facts of the truth of a proposition he has asserted in the pleadings. It is not the burden of production.

*burden of production = burden to come forward w/ evidence to support ā claim.*

3) The "true doubt" rule runs afoul of the APA, which provides that when the evidence is evenly balanced, the claimant must lose.

## L. ILLEGAL EVIDENCE

**1.** **Exclusionary Rule.** The exclusionary rule, which prohibits the use of illegally obtained evidence in criminal proceedings, is not necessarily applicable in agency proceedings. Traditionally, it was assumed that the rule applied. In *INS v. Lopez-Mendoza*, 468 U.S. 1032 (1984), the Supreme Court applied a cost-benefit analysis and concluded that the rule need not apply in all administrative proceedings. The states have the option of applying the rule to their own administrative proceedings.

*Deportation case ↳ clear, unequivocal & convincing evidence ↑ BOP*

**2.** **Types of Proceedings in Which Exclusionary Rule Applies--Powell v. Secretary of State,** 614 A.2d 1303 (Me. 1992).

Powell v. Secretary of State

**a.** **Facts.** Powell (P) was operating a vehicle that turned around before reaching a roadblock that had been set up to detect people driving under the influence of alcohol. He was pursued and stopped, then arrested for driving under the influence. At P's trial, the district court held that the evidence obtained following the stop, including the blood alcohol test, should be suppressed because the arresting officer lacked a reasonable suspicion of criminal activity to justify the stop. The secretary of state (D) suspended P's driver's license based on the arrest report and the blood alcohol test. P requested an administrative hearing. The hearing examiner refused P's request to exclude the evidence and upheld the license suspension. P appealed to the courts. The superior court vacated the hearing examiner's decision on the ground that the license suspension was "quasi-criminal" and the exclusionary rule should apply. D appeals.

  **b.** **Issue.** Does the exclusionary rule apply to an administrative license suspension hearing?

  **c.** **Held.** No. Judgment reversed.

   1) The exclusionary rule is a judicially created remedy intended to protect Fourth Amendment rights by deterring unlawful police conduct. This remedy has generally been limited to criminal cases, and the Supreme Court has never applied it in civil proceedings, except in "quasi-criminal" proceedings where a civil forfeiture of property is based on criminal conduct.

   2) The Supreme Court has set forth a balancing test for deciding what types of proceedings the exclusionary rule should be applied in. [*See* INS v. Lopez-Mendoza, *supra*] This test balances the likely social benefits of excluding evidence flowing from an unlawful seizure against the likely costs and benefits of using such evidence in a civil proceeding.

   3) In this case, the evidence has already been excluded from P's criminal proceeding, so there is little additional deterrent effect on police conduct by preventing consideration of the evidence at the administrative hearing. On the other hand, the costs to society of not allowing an administrative license suspension is great; the public has a substantial interest in eliminating the threat posed by persons operating motor vehicles while intoxicated.

   4) License suspension hearings are not quasi-criminal proceedings; they are reasonable regulatory measures to protect public safety. Applying the exclusionary rule to such proceedings would complicate and burden the process, which is designed to focus on the sole issue of whether a person was driving a vehicle with excessive alcohol in his blood.

**M. EXCLUSIVENESS OF RECORD**

 **1.** **General Rule.** When formal adjudication is required, it is incumbent on the agency to limit its consideration to evidence adduced on the record. However, this does not necessarily mean that a stenographic transcript of the hearing must be prepared.

2. **Tape Recordings as Official Record--Gearan v. Department of Health and Human Services,** 838 F.2d 1190 (Fed. Cir. 1988).

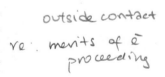

Ct upheld use of tape recording

   a. **Facts.** The Merit Systems Protection Board ("MSPB") had a procedure for tape recording its hearings, and it considered the tape to be the official record of the proceeding. The MSPB would make a copy of the tape recording, or transcript if prepared, of the hearing available to parties after payment of costs. The MSPB would make a written transcript at the requesting party's expense. Gearan (P) was a party to an administrative hearing with the Department of Health and Human Services (D). P appealed the MSPB's decision and now moves for an order directing the MSPB to prepare and file a written transcript of the hearing at its own expense.

   b. **Issue.** May an administrative board be required to prepare a written transcript of proceedings at its own expense upon the request of a party?

   c. **Held.** No. Motion denied.

      1) The APA requires an administrative agency to create and maintain transcripts of their hearings. The term transcript means "a copy of any kind," and this requirement has been interpreted to be satisfied by a tape recording.

      2) The MSPB normally provides a hearing tape when the court orders transmission of the record. The MSPB's policy provides for the MSPB to arrange for transcription into written format, at its own expense, if a court finds the tapes unsatisfactory. But there is no requirement that the MSPB create a written transcript at its own expense solely upon the request of a party.

   d. **Comment.** Tape recorded transcripts are increasingly common among administrative boards, although many still provide verbatim stenographic transcripts.

3. **Ex Parte Communications.** In formal adjudication, communications between the agency decisionmakers and the parties are prohibited unless all parties are provided with adequate notice thereof, and an opportunity to participate therein. Any ex parte communications must be summarized promptly by agency decisionmakers participating in them, and these summaries must be placed in the record. [APA §557(d)]

outside contact re: merits of c̄ proceeding

   a. **Basis of decision.** The prohibition against ex parte communications enhances the likelihood that the agency decision will have an adequate basis in fact.

   b. **Accuracy.** The rule also ensures that opposing parties will be able to challenge the accuracy of the assertions.

c.   **Judicial review.** On appeal, the courts can better evaluate the reasonableness of the agency's decision.

Banegas
v. Heckler

4. **ALJ's Own Observations--Banegas v. Heckler,** 587 F. Supp. 549 (W.D. Tex. 1984).

*Why exclusiveness of record (pp 571)*

a.   **Facts.** Banegas (P) applied for disability insurance benefits. His claim was denied, and on appeal the ALJ also denied P's claim. Although the evidence in the record overwhelmingly supported P's claim, the ALJ had followed P outside after the hearing and observed that P walked unimpeded. The appeals council affirmed the denial, despite P's attorney's affidavit that contradicted the observations by the ALJ. P sued Heckler (D), the Secretary of Health and Human Services, for review of the denial.

b.   **Issue.** May an ALJ act as a witness in a case he is hearing by performing his own investigation?

c.   **Held.** No. Judgment reversed.

1)   An ALJ acts as judge and juror in administrative hearings. He may properly observe a claimant during the hearing. However, he may not also act as a witness.

2)   The ALJ's conclusion in this case was based on matters outside the record. He put his own credibility in issue when he became a witness. His own observations contradicted the medical evidence, including the government's own medical expert. P is entitled to a new hearing.

N.   **OFFICIAL NOTICE**

1.   **Introduction.** Facts that are commonly known or that can be ascertained utilizing common reference sources may be referred to by administrative agencies. Ordinarily such facts must be set forth in the record, and opposing parties must be given an opportunity to rebut them. [APA §556(e)]

*In re* Griffith

2.   **Board Composed of Experts--*In re* Griffith,** 585 N.E.2d 937 (Ohio Ct. App. 1991).

*Board may rely on its own expertise b/c it possessed appropriate expertise & is capable of drawing its own conclusions + inferences*

a.   **Facts.** The Ohio Veterinary Medical Board held a hearing based on a complaint that Griffith (P), a veterinarian, had acted negligently in treating a kitten. At the hearing, P produced an expert witness who testified that P was not negligent in performing the operations, even though subsequent surgery was required to correct a mistake. The board nevertheless found that P was negligent and issued a written reprimand. P appealed to the court, but the decision was affirmed. P appeals.

**b.** **Issue.** May an administrative board composed of experts in the field substitute their own expert opinion for that of expert witnesses who testify at the proceeding?

**c.** **Held.** Yes. Judgment affirmed.

    1) In medical disciplinary proceedings, the board is composed of individuals with sufficient expertise and experience to consider whether a certain act is reasonable or a departure from minimal standards of care. There is no need for independent expert testimony where the board consists of experts in the field.

    2) If a party chooses, he may present expert testimony, but the board is not required to reach the same conclusion as the expert witness, even if that testimony is uncontroverted.

**3.** **Use of Guidelines Replacing Specific Findings--Heckler v. Campbell,** 461 U.S. 458 (1983).

Heckler v. Campbell

*upheld use of matrix guideline*

**a.** **Facts.** Social Security disability benefits are available to those whose disabilities render them unable to engage in any substantial gainful activity. The implementing regulations specified certain per se disabling impairments. Less severe impairments were evaluated by reference to medical-vocational guidelines instead of the former practice of relying on vocational experts. Campbell (P) applied for disability benefits. Although she was unskilled and had a limited education, and her physical condition prevented her from continuing her work as a hotel maid, the ALJ relied on the medical-vocational guidelines to determine that P could perform a significant number of jobs, so she was not disabled. On appeal, the court of appeals held that although the ALJ's determination was supported by the record, the medical-vocational guidelines did not provide specific evidence demonstrating that jobs were available for P. Because P was thus deprived of an opportunity to show she could not perform the jobs included in the guidelines, the determination of nondisability was not sufficient. Heckler (D), the Secretary of Health and Human Services, appeals.

**b.** **Issue.** May an administrative agency use guidelines to determine a claimant's rights to benefits instead of making specific findings for each case?

**c.** **Held.** Yes. Judgment reversed.

    1) The court of appeals required D to provide specific evidence of appropriate jobs for each claimant denied benefits. This holding implicitly questions the validity of the medical-vocational guidelines.

When an agency takes official or administrative notice of facts, a litigant must be given an adeq. opportunity to respond.

Except: when ē agency has promulgated valid regulations

Its purpose is to provide a procedural safeguard: to ensure ē accuracy of ē ~~three~~ facts already has been tested fairly during rulemaking. ē rulemaking proceeding itself provides sufficient procedural protection

2) Although disability determinations must be individualized, D may rely on rulemaking to resolve certain classes of issues. Otherwise the agency would have to relitigate continually issues that could be resolved fairly and efficiently in a rulemaking proceeding.

3) Under the law, D must first assess each claimant's individual abilities and then determine whether appropriate jobs exist. The first step requires a hearing because the issue is unique to each claimant. The second step pertains to the types and numbers of jobs in the economy, which does not vary with each claimant. This is a factual issue that can be fairly resolved through rulemaking. D's guidelines are not arbitrary and capricious and they do not conflict with the statute.

4) The principle that a claimant must have an opportunity to respond does not apply to rulemaking, which has its own procedural protections.

## O.  DECISION PROCESS

1. **Institutional Decisionmaking.** Typically, an agency's decision is the collective work product of several individuals. One hears the evidence, while another might sift the evidence and advise the decisionmaker, who signs an opinion with which he may have only casual familiarity.

2. **"The One Who Decides Must Hear."** The individual who is designated to decide the case must actually consider the evidence and the positions of the parties. This person may employ subordinates to take the evidence, sift and analyze it, but he must make the ultimate decision based on the evidence.

Morgan v.
United States
(PRE-APA)

Institutionalb decision (pp 589)

- typical decision in ē Admin process.

- ID is ē decision of ē agency as an admin entity rathen than ē personal decision of a known ind. admin.

3. **Requirement that Evidence Be Considered--Morgan v. United States,** 298 U.S. 468 (1936).

   a. **Facts.** The Secretary of Agriculture established the appropriate maximum prices for the purchase and sale of livestock in the Kansas City Stock Yards. Morgan and other affected parties (Ps) challenged the order, alleging that it was constitutionally infirm on the grounds that the Secretary had neither read the evidence nor heard the oral argument nor considered the briefs, but had merely consulted with his employees. The district court dismissed the suit. Ps appeal.

   b. **Issue.** Must the individual charged by the statute to make the decision actually consider the evidence?

   c. **Held.** Yes. Judgment reversed and case remanded.

1)     The Secretary is required by law to conduct a "full hearing," which is a proceeding of a quasi-judicial character. The term refers to the judicial tradition of having the trier of fact receive and weigh evidence, together with argument by the parties. If the one who determines the facts does not consider the evidence and argument, no hearing has been given.

2)     The decisionmaker may, however, delegate to subordinates the tasks of prosecuting inquiries, taking evidence, and sifting and analyzing it. But to provide the substance of a hearing, the officer who makes the determinations must consider and appraise the evidence that justifies them.

d.   **Comment.** This case continued to "yo-yo" up to the Supreme Court on four separate occasions. While the Court said that the "one who decides must hear," it broadly embraced the notion that a subordinate hearing examiner may actually "hear" the examination and cross-examination of witnesses and oral argument.

e.   *Morgan II.* On remand, Ps attempted to demonstrate that D had given the evidence insufficient consideration. In district court, Ps submitted more than 100 interrogatories and subjected D to elaborate depositions. One judge described D's efforts to evaluate the evidence and argument as "casual and perfunctory in the extreme." The Supreme Court in *Morgan II* stated that it was not the function of the Court to probe the mental processes of the Secretary in reaching his conclusions, but dodged this difficult question by deciding the case on other grounds. [Morgan v. United States, 304 U.S. 1 (1938)]

f.   *Morgan IV.* On remand, D was again subjected to oral and written interrogation concerning his mental processes. The Supreme Court objected to this treatment, concluding that D's function was analogous to that of a judge: "Just as a judge cannot be subjected to such scrutiny . . . so the integrity of the administrative process must be equally respected. . . ." [United States v. Morgan, 313 U.S. 409 (1941)]

*cannot be made to testify about their mental processes & how they reach their decision.*

g.   *Morgan* **criticism.** Some observers have concluded that although *Morgan I* establishes the principle that the one who is responsible for a decision must actually make it, *Morgan IV* appears to place a decisionmaker's method of rendering a decision beyond the realm of judicial scrutiny. [*See* KFC Management Corp. v. NLRB, 497 F.2d 298 (2d Cir. 1974)]

4.   **Hasty Decisionmaking.** Courts appear to be split on the question of whether a suspiciously swift agency resolution of complex issues renders the decision beyond *Morgan I.*

New England
Telephone &
Telegraph
Co. v. Public
Utilities
Commission

(PRE-APA)

5.  **Presumption of Propriety--New England Telephone & Telegraph Co. v. Public Utilities Commission,** 448 A.2d 272 (Me. 1982).

    a.  **Facts.** The New England Telephone & Telegraph Co. (P) sought increased revenues by filing revised tariffs with the Public Utilities Commission (D). After conducting hearings, D's examiners issued a report. P had six days to file exceptions, and D issued its final order denying P's request eight days after that deadline. P appeals, claiming that D did not independently consider the evidence because it was impossible to examine the evidence in eight days and because the final order was an almost verbatim reiteration of the examiner's report.

    b.  **Issue.** Does a short time interval between presentation of evidence and the issuance of a final order constitute evidence that an administrative agency has not independently evaluated the evidence?

    c.  **Held.** No. Judgment affirmed.

        1)  Courts must presume, in the absence of clear evidence to the contrary, that administrative agencies properly discharge their official duties. P's case is based on the inference that D did not independently evaluate the evidence and make the decision because of the short time interval between the examiner's report and the final order.

        2)  Due process does not require that officials who must make a decision must also read or hear all the testimony. They may be aided by reports prepared by subordinates. The purpose for hearing examiners is to aid D. The fact that D essentially adopted the examiners' report and did so within a relatively short time does not justify an inference that D committed improprieties.

6.  **Excessively Hasty Resolution.** However, at least one court has found an agency decision to be too hasty. The New York State Liquor Authority revoked a liquor license one hour after the conclusion of hearings (conducted by a subordinate) that had lasted three days. The agency decision was reversed on grounds that it failed to comply with its own regulations requiring that a stenographic record of the hearing be reviewed. [Weeks v. O'Connell, 304 N.Y. 259 (1952)]

7.  **Right to Review Examiner's Report.** While there is no constitutional right to have the hearing examiner prepare a report of her recommended findings and conclusions, if she does prepare a report, the agency must afford the parties an opportunity to review it, and submit evidence and arguments to the contrary. [Mazza v. Cavicchia, 105 A.2d 545 (N.J. 1954)]

*Crawley & FCC follow APA 557 decision making process*

## P. APA DECISION PROCESS

*see → 557 process*

1. **Administrative Procedure Act.** The APA requires the presiding officer to issue a decisional report unless the agency requires that the record be certified to it. When the ALJ renders a decision, it becomes that of the agency unless appealed. Usually the ALJ must recommend a decision, and it becomes a part of the record. Parties may then file exceptions thereto prior to the ultimate decision. [APA §557(b)(c)]

   *Admin. agency not bound by ALJ's decision.*

2. **Appeal of ALJ's Initial Decision.** The APA gives the agency all of the powers that it would have had in rendering the initial decision. [APA §557(b)] Hence, it is by no means prohibited from reversing the ALJ's conclusion, even if such overruling is largely based upon the demeanor of key witnesses.

3. **Clearly Erroneous Rule Inapplicable to Agency Appeals--FCC v. Allentown Broadcasting Corp.,** 349 U.S. 358 (1955).

   FCC v. Allentown Broadcasting Corp.

   a. **Facts.** Both Allentown Broadcasting Corp. (P) and Easton Publishing Co. applied for a radio license for the same frequency. The hearing examiner of the FCC (D) recommended that P be granted the license, and Easton filed exceptions to the decision. D reversed the decision and granted the license to Easton. P appealed. The court of appeals reversed D and agreed with the examiner. It held that since the examiner's conclusion was based on the demeanor of the witnesses, it could not be overruled absent a "very substantial preponderance" of the evidence. D appeals.

   *mr : Little Boy Blue Learning*

   b. **Issue.** May the agency overrule the hearing examiner's decision when that decision is largely based on the credibility of the evidence?

   c. **Held.** Yes. Judgment reversed.

   *reviewing ct's deference is to agency not ē ALJ.*

   *However, ē cases require agencies to explain ō grounds for rejection of ē ALJ's initial decision or findings.*

   1) The court of appeals adopted the "clearly erroneous" standard applicable to federal courts. This is too stringent a standard for intra-agency appeals, and would constitute a drastic departure from prior administrative practice.

   d. **Comment.** A contrary rule would make it very difficult for agency heads to reverse subordinate hearing examiners who insisted that their decisions were based on observations of witness veracity.

4. **Nonspecialized Board Must Accept Hearing Officer's Findings-- Crawley v. Department of Highway Safety,** 616 So. 2d 1061 (Fla. Dist. Ct. App. 1993).

   Crawley v. Department of Highway Safety

   *some ct's/states don't follow ē fed. rules.*

   a. **Facts.** The Department of Highway Safety (D) notified Crawley (P) that he would be suspended for "willful violation of statutory au-

   *PERC cannot overturn ē ALJ w/o comp. substantial evidence.*

thority, rules, regulations or policies" because he failed to obtain written authorization before working an off-duty police detail. P appealed his suspension to the Public Employees Relations Commission ("PERC"). The hearing officer found that P's failure to obtain authorization was inadvertent and not intentional. D objected on the ground that failure to comply despite knowledge of the policy constituted willful conduct. PERC found that P acted willfully, explaining that the hearing officer's conclusion was incorrect. P appeals.

    **b.**    **Issue.** May a hearing board with no special expertise in the area reject its hearing officer's finding of fact if the finding is based on evidence in the record?

    **c.**    **Held.** No. Judgment reversed.

        1)    The determination regarding willfulness does not implicate policy issues, but can be proven with ordinary methods of proof. It is a factual determination.

        2)    PERC could not reject the hearing officer's finding unless there was no competent, substantial evidence from which the finding could reasonably be inferred.

**5.**    **Constitution May Require APA Procedures.** Courts have held that even if the agency's statute does not require APA formal adjudication, nevertheless the Constitution may insist upon on it. [Wong Yang Sung v. McGrath, 339 U.S. 33 (1950)]

**6.**    **Review Boards.** A number of agencies have established review boards as an intermediate intra-agency appellate body to review appeals of recommended decisions of ALJs. Review boards are composed of senior career government officials. Often, appeal to review boards is the last appeal of right. Appeal to the agency heads becomes discretionary.

Eads v.
Secretary
of Health
and Human
Services

*Not covered?*

**7.**    **Court Cannot Consider New Evidence During Judicial Review--Eads v. Secretary of Health and Human Services,** 983 F.2d 815 (7th Cir. 1993).

    **a.**    **Facts.** Eads (P) suffered from diabetes and extreme obesity. Claiming he cannot work because he must elevate his legs for several hours during each day, he applied to the Secretary of Health and Human Services (D) for Social Security disability benefits. P offered no medical evidence to support his testimony at a hearing before the ALJ. The ALJ denied P benefits. P then requested that the appeals council of the Social Security Administration exercise its discretion to review the ALJ's decision, and submitted a doctor's letter that supported P's testimony about not being able to sit. The council refused to review the decision. P sought judicial review. The district court refused to consider P's physician letter because it had not been before the ALJ. P appeals.

**b.**    **Issue.** In considering an appeal from an ALJ's decision, may a district court consider evidence not submitted to the ALJ?

**c.**    **Held.** No. Judgment affirmed.

    1)    The appeals council has discretion to review ALJ decisions denying benefits. If the council does not agree to review the decision, the ALJ decision becomes final and judicially reviewable. If the council does review the decision, the council's decision, based on all the evidence before it, becomes the final decision that is judicially reviewable.

    2)    This procedure differs from judicial certiorari because claimants such as P may submit new evidence to the council to support the review application. When this happens, the new evidence becomes part of the record that goes to the district court in the judicial review proceeding. But that does not mean the courts can consider the new evidence; the courts consider the ALJ's decision, the correctness of which depends on the evidence that was before the ALJ. If the courts considered evidence never submitted to the ALJ, they would no longer be reviewing cases but would become equivalent to the ALJ.

    3)    The procedure P could have followed to have the doctor's letter considered by the ALJ is a petition for reexamination by the ALJ. P did not file such a petition. P could also seek judicial review of the council's refusal to consider the case in light of the new evidence. Finally, P could have asked the court to remand the case to D for consideration of newly discovered evidence, but he elected not to.

    4)    Since the ALJ did not err in finding against P when the doctor's letter is not considered, the decision must be affirmed.

## Q.   DECISIONS AND FINDINGS

**1.**    **Delegation of Voting.** The delegation to subordinates of voting powers is generally disfavored, unless the decisionmaker is fully apprised of the factual and legal issues in dispute and has himself considered the evidence and the positions of the parties.

**2.**    **Findings and Reasons Requirement.** For formal adjudication, the APA requires that an agency decision provide a statement of "findings and conclusions, and the reasons or basis therefor, on all the material issues. . . ." [APA §557(c)] The findings requirement ensures that judicial review can be performed, inhibits imprudent agency decisionmaking, provides an explanation to the affected parties of the agency decision and its rationale, and provides guidance to those similarly situated. An ideal administrative order contains five components:

a. The fundamental value judgments of the agency dictated by its understanding of the legislative purpose;

b. The facts that have been adduced and that are relevant to the agency's decision;

c. The process by which such evidence has been evaluated;

d. An organization of the evidence in a rational way; and

e. A conclusion based on the theory developed, supported by the facts, concerning whether a proposed action is in furtherance of the purposes set forth in the statute, along with an explanation of any change in agency policy from former practice.

Babac v. Milk
Marketing
Board

3. **Participation by Speakerphone Not Allowed--Babac v. Milk Marketing Board,** 584 A.2d 399 (Pa. 1990).

a. **Facts.** The Milk Marketing Board (D) set minimum producer, wholesale, and retail prices for fluid milk products sold in a specific area. Prior to adopting milk price orders, D held a conference to hear comments and to vote on the orders after considering the comments. D had a requirement of a quorum of three to take actions. Only one member of D was physically present at the conference, attended by milk producers and other interested parties. The other members participated through a speakerphone. D's members voted unanimously to adopt the orders. Babac (P) challenges the orders on the ground that D could not hold an official meeting when only one member was physically present.

b. **Issue.** May an administrative agency take action when some of the legally required participants are not physically present but merely participate over a speakerphone?

c. **Held.** No. Orders vacated.

1) The legislative intent of the statutes governing D was to require the physical presence of D's members at meetings. Conducting a meeting by speakerphone impairs the public's right of participation.

2) Without the physical presence of the minimum quorum, D could not take any official action, so the orders must be vacated and remanded for reconsideration.

**4. Preparation of Detailed Findings and Conclusions Required--Adams v. Board of Review,** 821 P.2d 1 (Utah Ct. App. 1991).

Adams
v. Board
of Review

a. **Facts.** Adams (P) worked as a telemarketer for a year when she developed pain in her neck and right arm and shoulder. P consulted a physician who diagnosed her as having several painful physical conditions that he believed were probably caused by P's job duties. P sought compensation from the Workers' Compensation Fund. The Fund required P to undergo independent medical evaluation by specified physicians. These doctors found that P's problem was psychological. A hearing was held before an ALJ, who denied benefits. P appealed to the Board of Review (D), which upheld the ALJ's decision. P sued for judicial review.

b. **Issue.** When an agency makes findings of fact and conclusions of law, must it prepare detailed findings and conclusions that can be reviewed on appeal?

c. **Held.** Yes. Judgment reversed.

1) Courts can sustain administrative orders if the findings that support the orders are sufficiently detailed to show that the agency properly arrived at the findings and properly applied the governing rules of law to those findings. A court can only review agency findings that are sufficiently detailed and include enough subsidiary facts to disclose the steps by which the ultimate conclusion on each factual issue was reached. If the agency does not make adequate findings of fact, the reviewing court may conclude that the agency's findings are arbitrary and capricious.

2) In this case, D's findings are limited to one statement: "The preponderance of medical evidence in this case establishes that the applicant's various listed symptoms are not related to her work as a telemarketer." While causation is an element P must prove, D's unexplained conclusion that P failed to prove causation is arbitrary.

3) A finding that contains only ultimate conclusions is not a valid finding. Nor is a mere recitation or summary of the evidence presented. The fact finder must determine what actually occurred after considering the conflicting evidence.

4) D should have first made a finding identifying P's occupational disease or injury. It could not conclude that her condition was not caused by her employment if it did not first establish what her medical condition was. Second, D should have provided an explanation about how P failed to prove causation. Third, D should have made subsidiary factual findings that support its decision. Because D did none of these, the court cannot effectively review the case. On remand, D

Administrative Law - 103

must make adequate findings and conclusions and enter a new order based on those.

De St.
Germain v.
Employment
Division

5. **Full Explanation Required--De St. Germain v. Employment Division,** 703 P.2d 986 (Or. Ct. App. 1985).

   a. **Facts.** De St. Germain (P) worked as a health care professional before leaving his employer. P applied to the Employment Division (D) for unemployment compensation benefits. The employer objected and D made an administrative determination denying P benefits because he left work. P sought a hearing. The hearing referee made findings of fact that P had a kidney stone problem that could have affected his ability to fulfill assignments his employer gave him, but concluded that P voluntarily left work without good cause and that continued work was available. D adopted the referee's opinion and denied P benefits. P appeals.

   b. **Issue.** May an administrative decision be upheld by the courts if the agency does not fully explain its decision?

   c. **Held.** No. Judgment reversed.

      1) The evidence shows that P experienced "horrible" kidney stone pain shortly before he left. His employer knew that P's problem could present a risk to his patients and offered P alternative work, which involved lifting patients. P declined the offer because lifting aggravated the kidney stone condition. There was other evidence tending to show that P's job safety concerns were legitimate.

      2) In light of the conflicting evidence, it is important that D explain its conclusions. But D's referee did not explain why P's alleged reasons for wanting to work elsewhere were not compelling. There were many possible reasons why they were not compelling, but the referee's brief explanation, without any legal reasoning, does not provide any basis for review. Accordingly, the case must be remanded.

R. **RECONSIDERATION**

   1. **Introduction.** The APA provides that a losing party may petition an agency to reconsider its decision or to reopen the proceeding. The agency has discretion to consider such a petition. A court normally does not review the agency's exercise of this discretion, but it is less clear whether a court may review an agency's refusal to review a case for abuse of discretion where there is new evidence or a change of conditions.

2. **Unreitable Order--ICC v. Brotherhood of Locomotive Engineers,** 482 U.S. 270 (1987).

a.  **Facts.** The Brotherhood of Locomotive Engineers (P) opposed certain proposed mergers between railroad companies. Other railroads also opposed the mergers, but sought trackage rights as tenants to hundreds of miles of the new consolidated railroads' track. The ICC (D) issued an order approving the mergers and granting the requested trackage rights. Parties have 60 days to petition for judicial review, but P did not raise a question about the impact D's order would have on crewing of the tenant railroads' trains. Several months later, P filed a petition for clarification that D's order did not authorize the tenant carriers to use their own crews on routes they had not previously served. D denied the petition on the ground that its order did allow the tenant railroads to use their own crews on these routes. P sought reconsideration and claimed that the tenant railroads' crewing procedures was a unilateral change in working conditions in violation of the Railway Labor Act. D denied the petition, and P sought judicial review of this denial within the 60 days.

b.  **Issue.** When an agency denies rehearing of a prior order, may a court when asked to review the denial review the prior order?

c.  **Held.** No. Petition denied.

    1)  D has authority to reopen and reconsider its prior actions, whether on its own initiative or upon petition by any interested party. When D reopens a proceeding and issues a new and final order, even if it merely reaffirms the rights and obligations of the original order, the new order is reviewable on its merits.

    2)  In this case, D refused to reopen the prior proceeding. The only thing left for a court to review is the lawfulness of the refusal. But an agency is not required to reopen a proceeding, so the only possible claim is that the refusal to reopen was arbitrary, capricious, or an abuse of discretion. To succeed under this standard, P would have to show new evidence or changed circumstances that make the original order inappropriate.

    3)  Instead, P here claims only "material error." To allow a court to review a prior order on this basis would eliminate the 60-day limitation provision by making review perpetually available, and on the same basis that an appeal within the original 60-day period would have involved. Since P's petition for reopening did not allege new evidence or changed circumstances, D's denial of the petition is nonreviewable.

# VII. JUDICIAL REVIEW

## A. INTRODUCTION

The essential purpose of judicial review is to serve as a check on the abuse of power or discretion by administrative agencies. Two essential issues must be raised: (i) Is review available? and (ii) What is the scope of review?

## B. STATUTORY SILENCE

1. **Nonstatutory Review.** Even where the legislature has not explicitly provided for judicial review (which it usually does), the absence of statutory authority for review has usually not been interpreted by the courts as constituting preclusion of review.

Stark v. Wickard

2. **Presumption of Availability of Judicial Review--Stark v. Wickard,** 321 U.S. 288 (1944).

   a. **Facts.** Wickard (D), the Secretary of Agriculture, established minimum rate orders governing marketing of milk in Boston. No explicit statutory provision provided for judicial review of such an order. Nevertheless, several producers of milk (Ps) brought an action in the district court to enjoin D from enforcing the order. The district court dismissed the complaint for failure to state claim upon which relief could be granted. The court of appeals affirmed. Ps appeal.

   b. **Issue.** Does the absence of statutory authority preclude judicial review?

   c. **Held.** No. Judgment reversed.

      1) The statute created an interest in Ps in minimum price regulation by D. Such an interest is capable of judicial resolution. Moreover, there is no forum other than the courts to hear the complaint.

      2) When personal rights are created by statute, silence as to judicial review is not to be construed as a denial of judicial relief, particularly when the matter is of a type typically resolved in the courts.

      3) When the legislature confers jurisdiction upon an agency, the agency's power is circumscribed by the perimeters of the statutory authority. Courts may properly review agency behavior to the extent necessary to protect an individual interest against agency excesses.

## C. STATUTORY PRECLUSION

1. **Narrow Construction.** Preclusion statutes are narrowly construed as a general rule.

2. **Administrative Procedure Act.** Under section 702, "a person suffering a legal wrong because of agency action, or adversely affected or aggrieved . . . is entitled to judicial review thereof."

3. **Filing Fees.** Reasonable filing fees do not constitute an unconstitutional violation of an appellant's rights to judicial review.

4. **Review Despite Statutory Preclusion--Department of Environmental Protection v. Civil Service Commission,** 579 N.E.2d 1385 (N.Y. 1991).

   Department of Environmental Protection v. Civil Service Commission

   a. **Facts.** Daly, an employee of the Department of Environmental Protection (P), threatened and then punched Gibbs, a fellow employee, to keep Gibbs from pressing criminal charges against two other employees who had committed a racially motivated attack against Gibbs. P charged Daly with misconduct, and after a hearing, the ALJ recommended that Daly be dismissed. P adopted the findings and terminated Daly. Daly appealed to the Civil Service Commission (D). D reviewed the hearing transcript, reversed the decision, and ordered Daly restored to his position. P sought judicial review. The lower court upheld D's decision. P appeals.

   b. **Issue.** May a court review an agency's decision if the law specifies that the decision is final and conclusive and not subject to judicial review?

   c. **Held.** Yes. Judgment affirmed on the merits.

      1) The statute clearly expresses legislative intent to preclude judicial review of D's decisions. But judicial review cannot be completely precluded. The courts have a duty to ensure that the agency has not exceeded its authority or acted illegally or unconstitutionally. Also, judicial review is always available if a constitutional right is implicated.

      2) This form of judicial review provides an extremely narrow standard of review. The courts can only inquire whether an agency has not acted in excess of its authority or in violation of state law or the Constitution. The substance of the agency's decision is not reviewable.

      3) In this case, there is no indication that D's decision was unconstitutional, illegal, or outside D's jurisdiction.

5.  **Discretionary Termination Unreviewable--Webster v. Doe,** 486 U.S. 592 (1988).

    a.  **Facts.** Doe (P) was employed by the Central Intelligence Agency ("CIA") as a clerk-typist. He was promoted to the position of covert electronics technician. P voluntarily informed the CIA that he was a homosexual. P was placed on leave during an investigation, and then was asked to resign. He refused. After review of P's records, Webster (D) terminated P. P then sued in federal court, claiming a violation of the APA because D's act was arbitrary and capricious, and various constitutional violations. D moved to dismiss P's complaint because section 102(c) of the National Security Act ("NSA") precludes judicial review of D's termination decisions. The lower courts denied D's motion. The Supreme Court granted certiorari.

    b.  **Issue.** May a federal agency make employee termination decisions unreviewable by the courts?

    c.  **Held.** Yes. Judgment reversed.

        1)  APA sections 701 to 706 allow any person adversely affected by an agency action to obtain judicial review, so long as the challenged action is a final action. However, section 701(a) limits application of the entire APA to situations in which (i) judicial review is not precluded by statute (an intent by Congress to prohibit judicial review) and (ii) the agency action is not committed to agency discretion by law (so that there is no law or standard for a court to apply).

        2)  Section 102(c) of the NSA allows D to terminate an employee whenever D "shall deem such termination necessary or advisable." This standard clearly defers to D and forecloses the application of any meaningful judicial standard of review. Implementation of section 102(c) was "committed to agency discretion by law," and D's actions pursuant to section 102(c) cannot be judicially reviewed.

        3)  D claims that judicial review of P's constitutional claims is also precluded by section 102(c). However, if Congress intends to preclude judicial review of constitutional claims, it must make its intent clear, and the NSA does not clearly express such an intent. On remand, the district court should address P's constitutional claims.

D.  **APA AND REVIEW OF DISCRETION**

    1.  **Administrative Procedure Act.** The APA allows judicial review except to the extent statutes preclude review, or the agency's determination is

committed to its discretion by law. [5 U.S.C. §701] Preclusion of review is limited to those situations where agency action is reasonable rather than arbitrary. Thus, although an agency action may be committed to its discretion by law, review is permitted where the agency abuses its discretion. [5 U.S.C. §706(2)(A)]

2.  **Action Committed to Agency Discretion.** The APA has been construed to mean that agency decisionmaking may be precluded if committed to its discretion by law only if the exercise of discretion is reasonable. Stated differently, the courts may properly reverse agency action for abuse of discretion. The exception for action committed to agency discretion has been described as rather narrow, and exists in those rare circumstances where the statutes are drawn in such broad terms that in a given case there is no law to apply.

3.  **Presumption.** There is a strong presumption favoring the availability of judicial review.

4.  **Agency's Discretion to Refrain from Enforcement--Heckler v. Chaney, 470 U.S. 821 (1985).**

Heckler<br>v. Chaney

   a.  **Facts.** Chaney and other death row inmates (Ps) petitioned the FDA to enforce its rules against use of drugs for unapproved purposes. Ps claimed that the drugs used for lethal injection had not been FDA approved for that use. The FDA responded that its jurisdiction over human execution was unclear but that, in any case, the FDA had authority to decline enforcement. Ps then sued Heckler (D), Secretary of Health and Human Services, seeking enforcement of FDA regulations. The lower courts ordered enforcement and the Supreme Court granted certiorari.

   b.  **Issue.** Do administrative agencies have discretion not to exercise their enforcement authority?

   c.  **Held.** Yes. Judgment reversed.

      1)  The APA permits judicial review of any agency final action, including a failure to act. The exceptions found in section 701(a) are (i) when statutes preclude agency review and (ii) when agency action is committed to agency discretion by law. D claims the latter exception applies.

      2)  The section 701(a)(2) exception is a narrow one, intended to apply only when statutes are written in such broad terms that courts have no standards by which to judge the agency's exercise of discretion. This interpretation is consistent with section 706(2)(A), which permits judicial review of abuse of discretion.

      3)  When an agency refuses to take enforcement action, the courts must presume that judicial review is not available. A decision not to pros-

ecute or enforce is a decision normally committed to an agency's absolute discretion. Such decisions are not suitable for judicial review for several reasons: (i) the decision involves agency expertise in performing a difficult balancing of factors; (ii) an agency normally cannot enforce every violation and must choose those where its resources are best used; (iii) an agency's refusal to act does not constitute exercise of coercive power over individual liberty or property rights; and (iv) the decision not to enforce is similar to a prosecutor's decision not to indict, which is within the special province of the executive.

## E.   STANDING

1.   **Justiciability.** Article III of the United States Constitution limits judicial power to the resolution of cases and controversies. This is the source of the standing requirement.

   a.   **Basic requirements.** One who seeks judicial review must allege that he has suffered some actual or threatened injury as a result of the illegal conduct of the defendant, that the injury is fairly traceable to the defendant's actions, and that it is likely to be remedied by a favorable decision. These requirements tend to assure that an actual case or controversy exists, and that the court will not be adjudicating some abstract issue. The dispute must be presented in an adversary context and in a form capable of judicial resolution.

   b.   **Nature of interests.** The concept of standing has been expanded in recent years to include adjudication of injury to a multitude of interests beyond those normally recognized at common law, including economic, aesthetic, and recreational interests.

Air Courier
Conference
v. Postal
Workers Union

2.   **Zone of Interests Protected by Statute--Air Courier Conference v. Postal Workers Union,** 498 U.S. 517 (1991).

   a.   **Facts.** The Private Express Statutes ("PES") codified the Postal Service's postal monopoly. The purpose of the PES is to prevent private competitors from offering service on low-cost routes, which would leave the Postal Service only the high-cost routes. The PES allows the Postal Service to suspend restrictions on any mail route "where the public interest requires suspension." The Postal Service suspended restrictions for "extremely urgent letters," which allowed private courier services to provide overnight delivery of letters. Relying on that suspension, members of the Air Courier Conference (D) used private courier systems to deposit letters sent to foreign addresses directly with foreign postal systems, a practice called "international remailing." The Postal Service issued a final rule permitting such international remailing. The Postal Workers Union (P) challenged the rule in federal court, claiming the rulemaking record was inadequate to support the finding that the rule was in the public interest. The district court granted summary judgment for D. The court of appeals vacated on the ground that the Postal Service relied on too narrow an interpretation of the "public interest." The Supreme Court granted certiorari.

b.  **Issue.** When an agency is authorized to suspend statutory restrictions on private companies that prevent them from competing with the government if the suspension is in the public interest, are agency employees whose jobs are adversely affected by the suspension within the zone of interests encompassed by the statutory restrictions?

c.  **Held.** No. Judgment reversed.

   1)  To establish standing, P must show that it has suffered a legal wrong because of the challenged agency action, or is adversely affected or aggrieved by the agency action within the meaning of a relevant statute. Then it must show that it is within the zone of interests sought to be protected through the statute.

   2)  The district court found that P satisfied the injury in fact requirement because the increased competition could adversely affect P's members' employment opportunities, and this finding was not appealed.

   3)  The court of appeals found that P satisfied the zone of interest requirement because the revenue protective purposes of the PES relate to P's interest in preventing the reduction of employment opportunities. But the language of the PES does not demonstrate congressional intent that postal workers were to be within the zone of interests protected by the PES. Congress was concerned with the receipt of necessary revenue for the Postal Service to perform its duties, not with opportunities for postal workers. The objectives of the grant of monopoly are to achieve national integration and to ensure that all areas of the country are served equally.

   4)  P notes that the Postal Reorganization Act ("PRA") contains a labor-management relations statute as well as the PES. Since the PES is the "linchpin" of the Postal Service, P claims employment opportunities are within the zone of interests covered by the PES. But the relevant statute in this case is the PES, because it is the one P alleges was violated, not the PRA, with all of its various provisions. None of the PES provisions have any integral relationship with the PRA's labor-management provisions. If the zone-of-interests test could extend to every provision in the PRA, it would lose virtually all meaning.

5)   P lacked standing to challenge D's order, and the courts should not have reached the merits of P's claim.

3.   **Statutory Authorization of Standing--Bennett v. Spear,** 520 U.S. 154 (1997).

   a.   **Facts.** Two Oregon irrigation districts that receive water from the Klamath Project and two ranches within those districts (Ps) seek judicial review of the decision of the Fish and Wildlife Service under the Endangered Species Act ("ESA") promulgating regulations that found that the Klamath Project water system was likely to jeopardize the existence of the Lost River and shortnose suckers. The district court and court of appeals held that they did not have standing.

   b.   **Issue.** Do Ps have standing under the citizen-suit provisions of the ESA and the APA to seek judicial review of the biological opinion in question?

   c.   **Held.** Yes. Judgment reversed and remanded.

      1)   The issue of standing involves constitutional limits on the exercise of federal court jurisdiction. In order for the case or controversy requirement to be fulfilled, a plaintiff must have suffered an injury in fact, that injury must be fairly traceable to the action of the defendant, and the injury must be capable of being redressed by a favorable decision.

      2)   The plaintiff's grievance must fall within the zone of interests protected or regulated by the statutory or constitutional provision at issue. The breadth of the zone varies according to the law at issue.

      3)   The ESA citizen-suit provision (which provides that "any person may commence a civil suit") negates the zone of interests test. The subject matter of the ESA is environmental protection, a matter in which all persons have an interest. Moreover, the ESA includes provisions authorizing litigation brought by private attorneys general, and eliminates the amount in controversy and diversity of citizenship requirements, thereby evincing an intention to open enforcement. This includes litigation brought by parties seeking to restrict environmental enforcement.

4.   **Public Interest Not Enough--Lujan v. Defenders of Wildlife,** 504 U.S. 555 (1992).

   a.   **Facts.** Section 7(a)(2) of the Endangered Species Act ("ESA") requires federal agencies to ensure, in consultation with the Secretary of the Interior, that any action carried out by such agency is not likely to jeopardize the continued existence of any endangered or threatened species. The Fish and Wildlife Service and National Marine Fisheries Service promulgated a joint regulation stating that section 7(a)(2) extended to actions taken in foreign nations, but the regulation was later modified to require consultations only for actions taken in the United States or on the high seas. The ESA also provided that "any person may commence a civil suit on his behalf" to enjoin a government agency that is alleged to be in violation of the Act. The Defenders of Wildlife (P) brought suit against Lujan (D), the Secretary of the Interior, seeking a declaratory judgment that the more recent regulation incorrectly interpreted the ESA. Both parties moved for summary judgment. The district court granted P's motion. The court of appeals affirmed. The Supreme Court granted certiorari.

b.    **Issue.** May Congress convert the public interest in proper administration of the laws into an individual right such that all citizens may have standing to sue?

c.    **Held.** No. Judgment reversed.

1)    Neither P nor any of its members had any injury in fact. P's standing, if any, depends on the validity of the "citizen-suit" provision of the ESA. The court of appeals held that this provision created a "procedural right" to inter-agency consultation in all persons, so that anyone can file suit to challenge D's failure to follow the allegedly correct consultative procedure, even if there is no discrete injury resulting from that failure. In effect, the court held that the injury-in-fact requirement under Article III has been satisfied by congressional conferral upon all persons of an abstract, self-contained "right" to have the Executive Branch observe the procedures required by law.

2)    Article III confers jurisdiction on the federal courts only when there is a case or controversy. This requirement is not met by a plaintiff raising only a generally available grievance about government, where the harm is only to the interest of all citizens in proper application of the Constitution and laws. Hence, a taxpayer does not have standing to challenge alleged violations of the Constitution by the Executive or Legislative branches if the violations would adversely affect only the generalized interest of all citizens in constitutional governance. The federal courts may only decide on the rights of individuals. Vindicating the public interest is the function of Congress and the President.

3)    If Congress could convert the undifferentiated public interest in an executive that complies with the law into an "individual right" to be vindicated in the courts, Congress could transfer from the President to the courts the Chief Executive's most important constitutional duty, to "take care that the Laws be faithfully executed."

4)    The fact that Congress may not eliminate the requirement of a concrete personal injury does not preclude Congress from creating legal rights, the invasion of which creates standing.

**d.** **Concurrence** (Kennedy, Souter, JJ.). Congress may define injuries and articulate chains of causation that give rise to a case or controversy where none existed before, but at a minimum, Congress must identify the injury it seeks to vindicate and relate the injury to the class of persons entitled to bring suit. The citizen-suit provisions of the ESA do not establish that there is an injury in any person by virtue of any violation. The case and controversy requirement ensures both that the parties have an actual stake in the outcome and that the legal questions presented will be resolved in a concrete factual context conducive to a realistic appreciation of the consequences of judicial action. The public is entitled to know what persons invoke the judicial power, their reasons, and whether their claims are vindicated or denied.

**5.** **Single Minor Event Does Not Confer Standing--Branton v. FCC,** 993 F.2d 906 (D.C. Cir. 1993).

**a.** **Facts.** National Public Radio ("NPR") broadcast a report on the trial of Gotti, the alleged leader of an organized crime syndicate, featuring a wiretapped telephone conversation that contained the "f-word" repeated 10 times. Branton (P) heard the broadcast and was offended. He filed a complaint with the FCC (D). D concluded that the broadcast was "not actionably indecent" and declined to take further action. P appealed, and D issued a letter ruling affirming the prior decision on the ground that the Gotti tape was part of a bona fide news story. P seeks judicial review.

**b.** **Issue.** Does a person obtain standing to challenge the FCC's failure to take action against a broadcaster if the person was offended by a single broadcast?

**c.** **Held.** No. Judgment affirmed.

1) P would have standing only if he alleged (i) a personal injury-in-fact that is (ii) fairly traceable to D's conduct and (iii) redressable by the relief requested.

2) In this case, P claims he was injured by being subjected to indecent language over the airwaves. Such a discrete, past injury does not confer standing on P, who does not seek relief for that harm but instead wants a sanction to prevent a repeat of such an offending broadcast. P's only continuing injury is the increased probabilities that, if D does not take action, he will be exposed in the future to similar indecencies. This marginally increased probability fails the "immediacy" requirement for standing. The possibility that NPR will again broadcast an indecency while P is listening is too remote to establish a case or controversy.

3) In *United Church of Christ v. FCC*, 359 F.2d 994 (D.C. Cir. 1966), the court held that responsible and representative groups in a broad-

caster's listening area have standing to challenge the broadcaster's application for a renewal license. But that case involved a continuing pattern of inappropriate broadcasting, which the FCC extended by renewing the broadcaster's license. P's claim in this case, which involves an isolated indecency, is entirely different.

4) P also cannot show that his injury is traced to the challenged action. D did not broadcast the obscenity. Even if D imposed a sanction against NPR, NPR could decide to broadcast such language again in the future. A reversal of D's decision thus may have no real consequence.

## F. PRIMARY JURISDICTION

1. **Relationship to Exhaustion.** Primary jurisdiction is closely related to the doctrine of exhaustion. Each involves the issue of whether further agency proceedings are required prior to judicial review.

2. **Exhaustion.** Exhaustion applies whenever the dispute is first cognizable solely in an administrative agency. The courts will defer action until the agency has concluded its proceedings.

3. **Primary Jurisdiction.** Primary jurisdiction involves a dispute that, although originally cognizable in the judiciary, requires resolution of certain issues within the special competence of an administrative agency. Here, judicial review is deferred until these issues have been first resolved by the agency.

   a. **Advantages.** The advantages of the application of the primary jurisdiction doctrine are:

      1) **Agency expertise.** The agency has been entrusted by the legislative branch to regulate a particular industry or area of public concern and has developed some expertise in the regulated affairs and application of the governing statute. The insights gained through agency experience and specialization may be useful in resolving complex issues of law or fact.

      2) **Uniformity.** Allowing the administrative agency an opportunity to decide all major issues surrounding the substance of its jurisdiction encourages uniformity of decisionmaking as well as stability and predictability in the law. These are objectives the legislature probably desired when it established the agency.

   b. **Disadvantages.** Referring questions to administrative agencies that the courts must ultimately review may only consume unnecessary time and money, and lead to less efficient and less economical decision-making.

<table>
<tr><td>Farmers<br>Insurance<br>Exchange v.<br>Superior Court</td><td>

**4.** **Discretionary Refusal to Exercise Jurisdiction--Farmers Insurance Exchange v. Superior Court,** 826 P.2d 730 (Cal. 1992).

**a.** **Facts.** The People, through the Attorney General, sued Farmers Insurance Exchange (P), alleging that P refused to offer a "Good Driver Discount policy" as required by state law. The People sought injunctive relief and in a second cause of action a civil fine based on the Business and Professions Code. P demurred on the ground that the People had failed to pursue and exhaust administrative remedies. The Superior Court (D) overruled the demurrer on the ground that the People could proceed under the Business and Professions Code despite the separate statutory scheme for enforcement of the Insurance Code. P sought a writ of mandate against D. The court of appeal affirmed on the ground that exhaustion of administrative remedies is not required before an action is brought under the Business and Professions Code. P appeals.

**b.** **Issue.** May a court exercise discretion under the primary jurisdiction doctrine to decline to hear a suit until administrative remedies have been exhausted, even if there is no statute that gives the court such discretion?

**c.** **Held.** Yes. Judgment reversed.

1) In *Texas & Pacific Railway v. Abilene Cotton Oil Co.*, 204 U.S. 426 (1907), the Supreme Court held that although the Commerce Act allowed a litigant to elect between administrative enforcement of statutory rights and judicial enforcement of common law rights, the statute should be interpreted to require litigants to invoke the administrative process first. Judicial actions should be limited to review of administrative actions and redress of such wrongs as can be redressed by courts without previous administrative action. The rationale was that the courts are not able to establish a uniform standard of rates without previous administrative action. This both preserves administrative autonomy to reach final decisions and promotes judicial efficiency by allowing the courts to take advantage of administrative expertise.

2) The *Abilene* doctrine has been further refined to require administrative action when the inquiry is one of fact and discretion in technical matters, and uniformity can be accomplished only when the determination is left to the administrative agency because of the expert and specialized knowledge of the agency. For example, in *Nader v. Allegheny Airlines*, 426 U.S. 290 (1976), the Court held that a plaintiff could bring a common law tort action for fraudulent misrepresentation against an airline that sold a confirmed ticket on

</td></tr>
</table>

an overbooked flight, even though the Civil Aeronautics Board was taking administrative action on such cases, because there was no need for expert or technical expertise to resolve the case.

    3)    Although P claims that the People should be required to exhaust administrative remedies, the applicable principle is the primary jurisdiction doctrine. Exhaustion applies when a claim is cognizable in the first instance by an agency alone, and the courts must wait until the administrative process is completed. Primary jurisdiction applies when a claim is originally cognizable in the courts, but requires resolution of issues that have been placed in the special competence of an agency. The judicial process is then suspended pending referral of the issues to the agency.

    4)    The Insurance Code establishes an administrative process for challenging insurance rates. The process includes procedures for investigation and resolution of complaints by the Insurance Commissioner, including public hearings, and also provides for judicial review. The law does not prohibit a court from exercising jurisdiction, but the courts should decline to adjudicate a suit until the administrative process has been invoked and completed. The People's complaint involves complex factual questions and technical issues regarding the Commissioner's own regulations that are within the expertise of the Commissioner and best left to him to decide in the first place. This promotes uniformity of decisions and benefits the courts when and if the case ultimately is reviewed in the courts.

**5.    Exception.** The rationale of agency expertise as a reason for applying the doctrine of primary jurisdiction has led to the creation of an exception where only a question of law is presented and no factual issue is in dispute. Thus, preliminary resort to the ICC was not deemed necessary in *Great Northern Railway v. Merchants Elevator Co.*, 259 U.S. 285 (1922), where the Court held that "the task to be performed is to determine the meaning of words of the tariff which were used in their ordinary sense and to apply that meaning to undisputed facts."

**6.    Agency Relief Unavailable.** Many federal courts have applied the doctrine of primary jurisdiction even when the agency has no power to provide the relief requested. However, a number of state courts do not apply the doctrine in such circumstances.

**7.    Primary Jurisdiction Applied--Far East Conference v. United States,** 342 U.S. 570 (1952).

    **a.    Facts.** The United States (P) brought an action in federal court alleging antitrust violations on behalf of the Far East Conference (D) and its member steamship companies for offering a two-tier price structure that dis-

Far East
Conference v.
United States

favored shippers who refused to use D's services exclusively in their trans-Pacific trade. D argued that the complaint should be dismissed until resort had first been made to the Federal Maritime Board ("FMB"). The district court found for D. P appeals.

b. **Issue.** Should the FMB rule on the question of the lawfulness of dual rates before the courts review it?

c. **Held.** Yes. Judgment affirmed.

1) The questions posed under the Shipping Act are highly technical and complex. They require the exercise of a high degree of expertise by those who, like the members of the FMB, are highly trained and experienced in such matters.

2) In cases raising issues of fact not within the conventional experience of judges, or cases requiring the exercise of administrative discretion, agencies created by Congress for regulating the subject matter should not be passed over.

3) Uniformity and consistency of decisionmaking are enhanced by preliminary resort to administrative agencies better equipped than courts to gain insight by specialization and experience.

## G. EXHAUSTION OF ADMINISTRATIVE REMEDIES

1. **Definition.** No one is entitled to judicial relief until the prescribed administrative remedy has been exhausted. Stated differently, a party may ordinarily not seek judicial review of administrative agency action until she has first utilized all her appellate opportunities within the agency.

2. **Rationale.**

a. **Avoidance of premature adjudication.** Like a trial court, the agency has been established to apply the statute in the first instance. It is usually desirable to allow the agency the first opportunity to develop the facts and apply the law.

b. **Administrative efficiency.** It is ordinarily more efficient to allow the agency to proceed without interruption than to allow judicial review at the various intermediate steps.

c. **Improved review.** Judicial review is enhanced by allowing the agency to develop a factual record and to apply its expertise. The judiciary can more efficiently deploy its resources by reviewing the agency record rather than compiling its own independent findings of fact.

d.  **Judicial efficiency.** A party who is forced to exhaust her administrative remedies may choose not to appeal an adverse judgment. Judicial interference in the administrative process would also weaken the agencies by encouraging parties to ignore those procedures.

3.  **Jurisdictional Challenges.** Parties who have objected to agency action on grounds that the action is ultra vires have had little success in the federal courts in securing judicial review of the jurisdictional question before the agency acts. They have had greater success in state courts.

4.  **The Futility of Appeals Exception--Portela-Gonzalez v. Secretary of the Navy,** 109 F.3d 74 (1st Cir. 1997).

    a.  **Facts.** Portela-Gonzalez (P) was a civilian employee at Roosevelt Roads Naval Station. In 1989, she placed 28 articles of clothing, worth $484.10, on lay-away at the Navy Exchange. When the Exchange later reduced the price, she cancelled the lay-away, and purchased the clothing for $330.79. For violation of Navy policies, the Navy (D) suspended her without pay. She contested the disciplinary action, and D terminated her employment. P appealed, and D affirmed its decision. P appealed again, was given a full evidentiary hearing, and D again affirmed her termination. She was given the opportunity for a final administrative appeal to the Deputy Assistant Secretary of the Navy. But rather than file this final appeal, she brought suit in federal court. The district court held that she had failed to exhaust her administrative remedies, but concluded that it had discretion to relieve her of the onus of this omission. Nonetheless, the court upheld P's termination.

    b.  **Issues.**

        1)  Has P failed to exhaust her administrative remedies?

        2)  If so, does the federal district court have discretion to ignore this failure?

    c.  **Held.** 1) Yes. 2) No. Judgment affirmed.

        1)  No one is entitled to judicial relief until the prescribed administrative remedy has been exhausted. This rule may be relaxed when: (i) unreasonable or indefinite delay threatens the subsequent bringing of the lawsuit, and the plaintiff will suffer irreparable harm if she is unable to secure immediate judicial resolution of her claim; (ii) substantial doubt exists as to whether the agency has the authority to grant meaningful relief; or (iii) there are clear, objectively verifiable indicia of administrative taint (such as where the decisionmaker is biased or has predetermined the issue).

Portela-
Gonzalez v.
Secretary
of the Navy

Exceptions.

2) P claims that the final appeal would have resulted in automatic affirmance of her dismissal, and would therefore have been futile. In order to prevail on a claim of futility, the plaintiff must show more than that she doubts that an appeal would result in a different decision; she must show that it is certain that her claim will be denied on appeal. This, P has failed to do.

3) Having found that P had failed to exhaust her administrative remedies, the district court was not then in a position to forgive the failure. The exhaustion doctrine exists to minimize cost and delay in the judicial system and avoid the waste of resources that would attend from premature adjudication.

Xiao v. Barr

5. **Agency Decides Its Own Jurisdiction--Xiao v. Barr,** 979 F.2d 151 (9th Cir. 1992).

a. **Facts.** Xiao (P) was paroled into the United States from China to testify at a criminal trial regarding a conspiracy to import heroin. When P testified that he had been tortured and coerced by the Chinese authorities into confessing falsely, the court declared a mistrial in the criminal case. P then sought declaratory and injunctive relief against the government (D) to prevent his return to China. The court granted relief pending final adjudication of P's request for asylum. When P's asylum request was denied, the INS placed him in administrative exclusion proceedings. P requested a hearing on his motion for partial summary judgment on the ground that the government could not remove him from the United States. The district court granted P summary judgment. D appeals, claiming the court lacked jurisdiction to enjoin exclusion proceedings.

b. **Issue.** May an administrative agency decide the question of its own jurisdiction to decide a case before it?

c. **Held.** Yes. Judgment reversed.

1) The Immigration and Nationality Act ("INA") provides that a court may not review an order of deportation or exclusion if the alien has not exhausted his administrative remedies. The district court concluded that P did not need to exhaust his remedies because he was not appealing an order of exclusion, but instead contesting D's authority to even place him into exclusion proceedings.

2) The exhaustion requirement of the INA has been interpreted to deprive a district court of jurisdiction until administrative remedies are exhausted, even when the alien is not seeking to attack a final order of exclusion. Exhaustion requires that D be accorded the opportunity to determine its own jurisdiction. It is no more circular to allow D to decide whether it has jurisdiction than it is for any court

to decide that it has jurisdiction when jurisdictional facts are also relevant to the merits.

3) The district court also claimed inherent supervisory powers to protect witnesses appearing before it, but these powers do not allow it to exercise jurisdiction in violation of the INA. D may consider the need to protect P in making its decision. P always can seek habeas corpus relief from any final order of exclusion. But since P has not exhausted his administrative remedies, the district court's injunction must be vacated, the summary judgment must be reversed, and the case must be remanded with directions to dismiss P's claims.

6. **Exhaustion of Administrative Remedies Not a Statutory Required Prerequisite--Darby v. Cisneros,** 509 U.S. 137 (1993).

Darby v. Cisneros

a. **Facts.** Darby (P), a real estate developer, obtained financing for certain projects and obtained mortgage insurance from Cisneros, the Secretary of the Department of Housing and Urban Development ("HUD") (D). P defaulted and D eventually had to pay over $6 million in insurance claims. D conducted an audit that concluded P had done nothing wrong, but D issued P a limited denial of participation in further projects administered by D. D also proposed a permanent debarment. P appealed D's actions, and an ALJ conducted a hearing. The ALJ concluded that a debarment of 18 months was appropriate. D's regulations provided that the hearing officer's determination is final unless D decides as a matter of discretion to review the findings or unless any party requests such a review. P did not seek further administrative review, but filed suit in federal court for an injunction and declaration that D's sanctions were imposed as punishment in violation of D's regulations. D moved to dismiss because P failed to exhaust administrative remedies. The district court denied D's motion, but the court of appeals reversed. The Supreme Court granted certiorari.

b. **Issue.** Must a plaintiff exhaust administrative remedies before seeking judicial review if neither the statute nor agency rules specifically mandate exhaustion as a prerequisite to judicial review?

c. **Held.** No. Judgment reversed.

1) APA section 10(c) provides that judicial review is available for final agency action, and that an agency action is final regardless of whether reconsideration has been sought unless the agency otherwise requires by rule. P claims that this means exhaustion is inapplicable unless specifically provided by the agency.

2) Section 10(c) pertains to finality, instead of directly to exhaustion, but it does establish when judicial review is available. Once an agency

action is final, it is subject to judicial review. Thus, section 10(c) limits the availability of exhaustion to that which the statute or rule clearly mandates. It would be inconsistent for courts to also require exhaustion of optional appeals.

3) The purpose of section 10(c) is to permit agencies to require appeals to superior agency authority before an examiner's initial decision becomes final. This reflects the pre-APA case law that agency action that was not administratively appealed was unreviewable because it was not yet final. But if an agency chooses not to require appeals, the APA provides that the initial decision is final and subject to judicial review. Courts are not free to impose an additional requirement of exhaustion when the action has become final under section 10(c). Accordingly, P was entitled to judicial review even though he did not exercise his option for further administrative appeals.

7. **Constitutional Challenges.** Exhaustion is sometimes not required when the constitutionality of the statute or the agency's act is challenged.

## H. RIPENESS FOR REVIEW

1. **Ripeness.** When one seeks discretionary relief from the judiciary of an agency action, the courts may resist review until the controversy is "ripe." This avoids premature adjudication of disputes that have not reached sufficient concreteness to warrant judicial interference, and avoids disruption of agency decisionmaking until the impact thereof has run its course.

2. **Liberalization of Ripeness.** The modern trend has been to relax the ripeness prohibition of discretionary judicial review. When the party is faced with an agency decision having immediate adverse effects, and the consequences for noncompliance are severe, courts have been willing to open the doors to judicial review.

3. **Premature Review.** If the consequences of agency action are not immediately felt, pre-enforcement judicial scrutiny may be denied. [*See* Toilet Goods Association v. Gardner, 387 U.S. 158 (1967)]

Dietary Supplemental Coalition v. Sullivan

4. **No Judicial Review of Preliminary Action--Dietary Supplemental Coalition v. Sullivan,** 978 F.2d 560 (9th Cir. 1992).

a. **Facts.** The Food and Drug Administration ("FDA") (D) issued regulatory letters concerning the dietary supplement CoQ10 informing recipients that CoQ10 was an unapproved food additive and that its sellers were subject to enforcement actions. The Dietary Supplemental Coalition (P), whose members sold CoQ10, sued for a declaratory judgment that their products are "foods" and not "food additives," or are "generally recognized as safe" under the Food and Drug Act. The district court dismissed the suit on the ground that the issues were not ripe for judicial review. P appeals.

**b. Issue.** May a party seek judicial review of an agency's preliminary action?

**c. Held.** No. Judgment affirmed.

1) There are two elements of ripeness: (i) the fitness of the issues for judicial decision, and (ii) the hardship to the parties of withholding court consideration. The fitness element requires that the issue involve a final agency action and be primarily legal with no further factual development required. The hardship requirement requires evidence of a direct and immediate hardship resulting from withholding judicial review.

2) The final agency action requirement is intended to avoid interference with an agency's decisionmaking process. Regulatory letters have been held not to constitute final agency action. D in this case has not made a statement regarding CoQ10 in general, but only with regard to its use in certain products. Classification of a product as "food" involves technical and scientific questions such that a court should decline review of anything less than a final agency determination on the classification. The classification of "foods" and "food additives" is a fact-based determination, not a purely legal one, and D can make that determination by taking a legal position in separate actions.

3) The trial court also found that P's risk of seizures and injunctions was too speculative to warrant judicial intervention. But since D has not made a final determination, P has not shown sufficient hardship to bypass final agency action by D. The most P has shown is that the pursuit of administrative remedies may be time consuming, but this is not a sufficient justification for invoking federal court jurisdiction.

**5. No Judicial Review Where Regulation Has Not Been Applied to the Plaintiff--Reno v. Catholic Social Services,** 509 U.S. 43 (1993).

Reno v. Catholic Social Services

**a. Facts.** Under the Immigration Reform and Control Act of 1986, an illegal alien could become a legal resident by proving continual residence in the United States since 1982 and physical presence since 1986. The Immigration and Naturalization Service ("INS") (D) issued a regulation providing that "brief, casual and innocent absences" from the United States would not disqualify an illegal alien, but only if the alien had obtained permission from the INS before leaving the country. Catholic

Social Services (P) brought a class action, challenging the regulation. The lower courts invalidated the regulation. D appeals.

**b.    Issue.** May a court review a challenge to an administrative agency's regulation in a case in which the regulation has not actually been applied against the plaintiff?

**c.    Held.** No. Judgment reversed.

1)    The Reform Act contains an exclusive scheme for administrative and judicial review of determinations on the status of aliens seeking resident status. There is one level of administrative appellate review, to be followed by judicial review only if there is an order of deportation.

2)    An adverse decision by the administrative appellate authority does not trigger deportation proceedings, but merely leaves the alien in the same position he was in before he applied for legalization; *i.e.,* he is an illegal alien. An order of deportation does not issue unless and until the alien either turns himself in or is caught by the INS. The alien can then appeal a deportation order to federal court.

3)    Nothing in the Reform Act precludes district court jurisdiction over an action challenging the legality of an INS regulation, even when there is no denial of any individual application. The APA also favors judicial review when someone claims an agency action caused a legal wrong. But a court may decline to take action in a suit for injunctive and declaratory judgment remedies if the controversy is not "ripe" for judicial resolution.

4)    To be "ripe" for review, the effects of the administrative action challenged must have been felt in a concrete way by the challenging parties. The promulgation of a regulation can affect parties concretely enough to make the controversy ripe, such as when the regulation forces the plaintiff to choose between a disadvantageous restriction and risking serious penalties for violation, as was the case in *Abbott Laboratories v. Gardner*, 387 U.S. 136 (1967).

5)    In this case, P's claim is not ripe. The INS regulations do not impose a penalty; they merely limit access to a benefit created by the Reform Act. The benefit is available only after taking affirmative steps, so an illegal alien's claim could ripen only once he took the affirmative steps that he could take before the INS blocked his path by applying the regulation to him. At that point, the alien can pursue the appellate procedures contained in the Act.

**d.    Concurrence** (O'Connor, J.). An anticipatory suit by a would-be beneficiary of a benefit-conferring rule, where the benefit has not yet been applied for, is a different ripeness issue than a pre-enforcement suit against a duty-creating rule. But such a suit is not necessarily unripe simply because the benefit has not been applied for. If it is "inevitable" that the challenged rule will operate to the plaintiff's disadvantage, then the suit might be ripe.

⟶ *Ripeness.*

Freedom
to Travel
Campaign
v. Newcomb

6. **The "Firm Prediction" Rule--Freedom to Travel Campaign v. Newcomb,** 82 F.3d 1431 (9th Cir. 1996).

    a. **Facts.** Freedom to Travel Campaign (P) challenged the constitutionality of a restriction against travel to Cuba imposed by the Treasury Department's (D's) Cuban Assets Controls Regulation. P never applied for permission to travel under the regulation's exemptions from the general rule of prohibition. The lower courts upheld the regulations.

    b. **Issue.** Does P have standing to challenge the regulations?

    c. **Held.** Yes. Judgment affirmed.

        1) The issue of ripeness turns on: (i) whether the issue is fit for judicial resolution; and (ii) whether the parties would suffer undue hardship if judicial review were denied. Legal issues that require little factual development are more likely to be deemed ripe.

        2) Here, the criminal penalties imposed by the regulations subject P to sufficient hardship. There is no reason for P's application to be first rejected before it may bring suit.

        3) This court adopts the "firm prediction" rule, under which, if the court can make a firm prediction that the agency will deny the party its sought relief under the regulation, there may be a justiciable controversy suitable for judicial resolution. We believe that we can firmly predict that D would deny P's travel request, and therefore, P's claim is ripe.

    d. **Concurrence.** Since P did not apply for, and suffer denial of, a license for travel to Cuba, it cannot challenge the statute and regulations on grounds other than First Amendment grounds. However, P's First Amendment claim is ripe for judicial review.

## I. TORT SUITS AS REVIEW ACTIONS

1. **Sovereign Immunity.** Sovereign immunity has been held to bar relief against a governmental official unless his action was either ultra vires or unconstitutional. The courts carved out these exceptions presumably under the fiction that such suits were not against the government, but against the individuals who committed the wrongs complained of. But in many

cases, in situations where the normal rules of agency would impose liability upon a principal for the actions of his agent, government officials have been immune from injunctive or declaratory relief under the doctrine of sovereign immunity.

2. **Federal Tort Claims Act of 1946.** The Federal Tort Claims Act provides for specific waiver of the defense of sovereign immunity for certain circumstances or agencies, specified torts, and discretionary acts by government employees. But there is generally no governmental liability for intentional torts.

Watts v.
Burkhart

3. **Quasi-Judicial Immunity--Watts v. Burkhart,** 978 F.2d 269 (6th Cir. 1992).

    a. **Facts.** Watts (P) was a medical doctor who prescribed Preludin for weight-loss programs. P was charged with malpractice and unprofessional conduct, and was notified of a hearing to be held before the Board of Medical Examiners. P appeared at the hearing without counsel and signed a "voluntary" surrender of a certificate from the U.S. Drug Enforcement Administration that permitted P to handle controlled substances. P later advised the Board that he desired to withdraw the surrender of the certificate. P then sued Burkhart and the other Board members (Ds) in their individual capacities. P claimed Ds violated P's due process and equal protection rights. P sought damages of nearly $2 million. Ds moved to dismiss, but the district court denied the motion. Ds appeal.

    b. **Issue.** Are the members of a state medical licensing board protected by quasi-judicial immunity when sued individually for damages in connection with the Board's suspension of a physician's license?

    c. **Held.** Yes. Judgment reversed.

        1) In *Bradley v. Fisher*, 80 U.S. (13 Wall.) 335 (1872), the Court held that the doctrine of judicial immunity protects judges from civil liability for their judicial acts, even when they allegedly act outside their jurisdiction. Prosecutors are likewise immune from liability for their official acts, as are members of a state bar grievance committee that recommends revocation of a plaintiff's license to practice law.

        2) Absolute immunity was extended to non-judges in *Butz v. Economou*, 438 U.S. 478 (1978). The Court noted that executive officials normally have only qualified immunity when charged with constitutional violations, but the absolute immunity for judges and prosecutors should extend to executive branch officials who act in quasi-judicial proceedings under the APA.

3)  Judicial immunity arises not because of which branch the official works in, but because of the characteristics of the process involved. It is intended to free the judicial process from the harassment and intimidation associated with litigation. A modern federal hearing examiner's role is functionally comparable to a judge's role.

4)  The same rule applies at the state level provided that the process has restraints and safeguards comparable to those provided by the APA. In this case, D's Board requires that its members be experienced, licensed physicians, appointed by the governor for fixed terms. They must conduct proceedings using the procedures set forth in the Uniform Administrative Procedures Act, which contains safeguards comparable to those in the APA. The Board clearly had jurisdiction over P.

5)  Finally, the Board satisfied the three-part test set forth in *Bettencourt v. Board of Registration in Medicine*, 904 F.2d 772 (1st Cir. 1990): (i) the Board must perform a traditional adjudicatory function by deciding facts, applying law, and resolving disputes on the merits, free from direct political influence; (ii) it must decide cases sufficiently controversial that, in the absence of absolute immunity, they would be subject to numerous actions for damages; and (iii) they must adjudicate disputes using procedures that protect the constitutional rights of those before them.

4.  **Discretionary Function Immunity--United States v. Gaubert,** 499 U.S. 315 (1991).

United States
v. Gaubert

a.  **Facts.** Gaubert (P) was the chairman of the Independent American Savings Association ("IASA"), a federally insured savings and loan. Officials at the Federal Home Loan Bank Board ("FHLBB"), a federal institution, wanted to have IASA merge with a failing Texas thrift, but were concerned about P's financial dealings and had him removed from the IASA management. P also had to post a $25 million interest in real property. The FHLBB officials then provided advice to facilitate the merger, but never instituted formal action against IASA. Subsequently, the FHLBB threatened to close IASA unless its directors resigned. They did so, and new management and directors took over. The FHLBB and its Dallas correspondent closely advised management in a variety of important matters. Shortly after they took over, the new directors announced that IASA had a substantial negative net worth. P filed an administrative tort claim with the federal agencies involved seeking $75 million for the lost value of his shares and $25 million for the property he lost under the guarantee he provided. P's claim was denied and he filed suit under the Federal Tort Claims Act ("FTCA"). The district court dismissed the suit on the ground that all of the challenged actions of the regulators fell within the discretionary function exception of the FTCA. The court of appeals affirmed in part but reversed in part on the ground that the regulators went beyond making policy-oriented decisions, which are immune under the FTCA, and provided operational actions by participating in IASA's management decisions. The Supreme Court granted certiorari.

**b.  Issue.** Are an agency's actions including participating in management of a regulated business exempt from liability under the FTCA "discretionary function" exception?

**c.  Held.** Yes. Judgment reversed.

1) The discretionary function exception protects the government against liability for actions of government employees who perform a discretionary function on the part of a federal agency, whether or not the discretion involved is abused. When the challenged conduct involves an element of judgment, the conduct is protected only if the judgment is of the kind the discretionary function exception was designed to shield.

2) If a regulation mandates particular conduct and the employee obeys the direction, the government is protected because the action furthered the policies that led to the promulgation of the regulation. If a regulation allows the employee discretion, the existence of the regulation creates a strong presumption that a discretionary act authorized by the regulation involves consideration of the same policies that led to the promulgation of the regulations.

3) A discretionary act involves choice or judgment, but it is not limited to policymaking or planning functions. Day-to-day management involves choice or judgment, and can also be based on policy. There is no reason to hold that management or operational activities are outside the scope of the discretionary function exception. Since P basically alleged negligence by federal officials in their participation in IASA's management, his claim is barred by the discretionary function exception to the FTCA.

## J.  SCOPE OF REVIEW

1. **Substantial Evidence Rule.** The Supreme Court announced the substantial evidence rule in *ICC v. Union Pacific Railway*, 222 U.S. 541 (1912). The rule provides that substantial evidence is more than a mere scintilla. It is such evidence as a reasonable mind might accept to support a conclusion.

**a.** **Insufficient evidence.** Mere uncorroborated hearsay or rumor is not substantial evidence. To be substantial, it must be sufficient to justify a refusal to direct a verdict if the case were before a jury.

**b.** **APA.** The substantial evidence rule is now codified in APA section 706(2)(E). It applies to a review of formal rulemaking or formal adjudication (where the proceeding is subject to APA sections 556 and 557 or otherwise "on the record").

**c.** **The whole record.** In determining whether an agency decision is supported by substantial evidence, courts must evaluate the whole record in its entirety, not merely those portions on which the agency relied.

**d.** **Duty of reviewing court--Universal Camera Corp. v. NLRB,** 340 U.S. 474 (1951).

Universal<br>Camera Corp.<br>v. NLRB

    **1)** **Facts.** The NLRB (D) ordered Universal Camera Corp. (P) to reinstate with back pay one of its employees found to have been fired because he had given testimony under the Wagner Act. The Wagner Act provides that "the findings of the Board as to the facts, if supported by evidence, shall be conclusive." The court of appeals affirmed the reinstatement order. P challenged the decision because, taken as a whole, the record did not support D's decision.

    **2)** **Issue.** Must the reviewing court assess whether the agency's decision is supported by substantial evidence upon the record considered as a whole?

    **3)** **Held.** Yes. Vacated and remanded.

        a) The Wagner Act's reference to evidence means "substantial evidence." Substantial evidence is "more than a mere scintilla. It means such relevant evidence as a reasonable mind might accept as adequate to support a conclusion." It must be sufficient "to justify, if the trial were to a jury, a refusal to direct a verdict."

        b) The Attorney General's Committee issued a report in 1941 on the predecessor to the APA. Three members registered a dissent in which they argued against the traditional interpretation of the substantial evidence test. The then-prevailing view was that the rule was satisfied if substantial evidence was found to exist anywhere in the record, irrespective of "how heavily the countervailing evidence may preponderate . . . " so that courts could merely examine one side of the case; if substantial evidence existed there, contrary evidence could be ignored and the agency's decision could be sustained. Presumably responding to this criticism, the proposed language was subsequently amended to include the phrase "upon the whole record." Congress unanimously embraced this language when it promulgated the APA in 1946.

c) The substantiality of evidence must take into account whatever in the record fairly detracts from its weight. This is clearly the significance of the requirement that "courts consider the whole record."

d) The lower courts must assume more responsibility for the reasonableness and fairness of agency decisionmaking than they have in the past. They must keep the agencies within reasonable bounds. An agency's decisionmaking must be set aside when the evidence is not substantial when viewed on the whole record. The substantial evidence test is the standard of review to be applied by the court of appeals.

d) The Supreme Court will intervene only where the standard has been misapprehended or grossly misapplied. Here, it appears that the court did consider the record as a whole. Therefore, the case will be remanded to the court of appeals to determine whether enforcement should be granted.

**4) Comment.** Note that substantial evidence review is one which essentially focuses on the reasonableness of the agency's conclusions. The agency will be upheld if its findings are reasonable, even if the court might have independently reached a contrary conclusion had the question been before it in the first instance. Note also that the court need not engage in weighing the evidence.

**e. Supreme Court review.** Although the scope of review for the courts of appeals for formal rulemaking or adjudication is "substantial evidence on the record as a whole," the Supreme Court "will intervene only where the substantial evidence standard has been misapprehended or grossly misapplied." [American Textile Manufacturers Institute v. Donovan, *infra*] Thus, the appellate court application of the review standard will likely be upheld unless it is patently unreasonable.

**f. Administrative Procedure Act.** The scope of review provision is APA section 702.

**1) Statutory and constitutional questions.** The APA provides that "the reviewing court shall decide all relevant questions of law, [and] interpret constitutional and statutory provisions. . . ." (*But see* discussion of the rational basis test, *infra*.)

**2) Substantial evidence.** As has been discussed, formal rulemaking and formal adjudication subject to APA sections 556 and 557 are subject to the substantial evidence test. [APA §706(2)(E)]

**3) Arbitrary and capricious.** Presumably, agency decisions not subject to APA sections 556 and 557 or otherwise "on the record" are subject to reversal or remand if found to be "arbitrary, capricious, an abuse of discretion, or otherwise not in accordance with the law. . . ." [APA §706(2)(A)]

**4)** **Unconstitutionality.** Of course no agency decision can sustain judicial scrutiny if it is unconstitutional. [APA §706(2)(B)]

**5)** **Ultra vires.** [APA §706(2)(C)]

**6)** **Procedural infirmities.** [APA §706(2)(D)]

**7)** **Trial de novo.** [APA §706(2)(F)]

**g.** **Limited Supreme Court review--American Textile Manufacturers Institute v. Donovan,** 452 U.S. 490 (1981).

American Textile Manufacturers Institute v. Donovan

**1)** **Facts.** The facts and first portion of the opinion are set forth *supra*.

**2)** **Issue.** In reviewing a lower federal court's review of an agency decision based on an alleged lack of substantial evidence, may the Supreme Court do more than determine whether the court misapprehended or grossly misapplied the substantial evidence test?

**3)** **Held.** No. Judgment affirmed.

a) The applicable Act places responsibility for determining substantial evidence questions in the court of appeals, so on review, the issue is not whether this Court would, in the first instance, find OSHA's findings supported by substantial evidence. Instead, this Court may examine OSHA's findings and the record on which they were based only to decide whether the court of appeals misapprehended or grossly misapplied the substantial evidence test.

b) In this case, OSHA relied in part on two cost estimates to determine whether its Cotton Dust Standard was "economically feasible." While there was considerable controversy about OSHA's use of the estimates, since OSHA essentially disregarded much of them and substituted its own judgment, the court of appeals applied the substantial evidence test and found that OSHA had reasonably evaluated the cost estimates, considered criticisms of each, and selected suitable estimates of compliance costs. Thus, it did not misapprehend or grossly misapply the substantial evidence test.

**4)** **Dissent** (Stewart, J.). OSHA clearly failed to justify its cost estimate on the basis of substantial evidence. The agency never relied on any study that purported to predict the cost of the standard OSHA finally adopted. Instead, it used a study of a different standard and did not rely on even a single estimate of the cost of its actual standard. OSHA's decision was based on unsupported speculation. This is a rare instance where an agency has misconceived the nature of the evidence necessary to support a regulation, and the court of appeals failed to correct that error.

**h.** **Reasons requirement--Citizens to Preserve Overton Park v. Volpe,** 401 U.S. 402 (1971).

    **1)** **Facts.** The Secretary of Transportation (D) authorized construction of an interstate highway through Overton Park in Memphis, Tennessee. The highway would consume 26 acres of the 342-acre city park. D made no formal findings explaining his decision and its consistency with federal statutes, but provided litigation affidavits asserting that the decision was his and was supportable by law. Federal legislation prohibited federal highway construction through public parks where a "feasible and prudent" alternative route exists. Citizens to Preserve Overton Park (Ps) contended that D did not make an independent determination. The district and appellate courts found that formal findings by D were not required, and Ps appeal.

    **2)** **Issue.** Does D's failure to explain the rationale for his decision or its consistency with federal statutes constitute error?

    **3)** **Held.** Yes. Judgment reversed and remanded.

        **a)** The case must be remanded so that the full record before D at the time he rendered his decision can be evaluated. There is no de novo review and D's approval of the highway does not have to meet the substantial-evidence test. However, the court must decide whether D acted within his scope of authority and whether his choice was "arbitrary, capricious, an abuse of discretion, or otherwise not in accordance with the law."

    **4)** **Comment.** This case is among the most frequently cited decisions in Administrative Law. Its facts depict a rather common practice in agency decisionmaking where subordinates are delegated the task of rendering many of the agency's technical decisions and the agency head dictates policy. The large number of decisions required by law to be made by administrative agencies makes such delegation necessary. But when it occurs, a prudent decisionmaker will have his subordinate prepare a written decision explaining the facts and their application to the law.

**i.** **Comparison between substantial evidence and arbitrary or capricious standards--Association of Data Processing Service Organizations v. Board of Governors,** 745 F.2d 677 (D.C. Cir. 1984).

    **1)** **Facts.** After a hearing held by an ALJ, the Board of Governors (D) of the Federal Reserve System issued two orders that had the effect of allowing bank holding companies to engage in data processing and transmission services. One order was adopted in an adjudicatory setting and the other after informal notice and comment rulemaking. The Association of Data Processing Service Organizations (P) sought review of these orders. The statute that permits judicial review states that D's findings as to the facts, if supported by substantial evidence, shall be conclusive.

2) **Issue.** In reviewing factual determinations, does the substantial evidence standard require the same scrutiny as the arbitrary or capricious standard?

3) **Held.** Yes. Orders upheld.

a)   Because different statutory sections apply to each type of proceeding, courts apply the arbitrary or capricious standard to D's rulemaking and the substantial evidence standard to D's adjudications. However, the language in the Bank Holding Company Act specifying the substantial evidence standard of review does not distinguish between rulemaking and adjudication.

b)   Despite varying approaches taken by courts that have interpreted this statute, the proper interpretation is to five general applications to the substantial evidence language. In fact, as applied to the requirement of factual support the substantial evidence test and the arbitrary or capricious test are the same thing. Any factual judgment not supported by substantial evidence would be arbitrary.

c)   The substantial evidence language as used in this statute requires the same amount of factual support as the substantial evidence provision of the APA, which is actually the same as that required by the arbitrary or capricious standard.

j.   **State scope of review.** Section 15(g)(5) of the Model State APA provides for judicial reversal of agency decisions that are "clearly erroneous in view of the reliable, probative, and substantial evidence on the whole record." However, the 1982 Model Act revokes the "clearly erroneous" standard in favor of the federal "substantial evidence" test.

2.   **Agency Delay--Heckler v. Day,** 467 U.S. 104 (1984).

Heckler
v. Day

a.   **Facts.** The Social Security disability program used a four-step process for review and adjudication of claims: (i) a state agency determines whether the claimant is disabled; (ii) a dissatisfied claimant may require reconsideration; (iii) if still dissatisfied, the claimant may obtain a de novo review by an ALJ; and (iv) if still dissatisfied, the claimant may appeal to the Department of Health and Human Services. The statute requires that hearings be held within a reasonable time. Day (P) had to wait almost six months between steps two and three. P brought a class action seeking declaratory and injunctive relief. After conducting a survey, the district court held that for all disability claimants in Vermont, delays over 90 days from a request for an ALJ hearing to the hearing itself were unreasonable. The court ordered Heckler (D), the Secretary of Health and Human Services, to comply with the 90-day deadline and to pay interim benefits to claimants who did not receive the hearing within that time. The court of appeals affirmed. D appeals.

b. **Issue.** May a court impose deadlines for agency action when it determines the delays are caused by inefficiency?

c. **Held.** No. Judgment reversed.

    1) D admits that hearings must be held within a reasonable time and that the delays P encountered were unreasonable. However, D claims the court abused its equitable power in imposing deadlines through a statewide injunction.

    2) Congress has considered the problem of delays but rejected mandatory deadlines as a cure. It has apparently decided that concern for the quality and uniformity of agency decisions outweighs the delay problem. Judicial imposition of deadlines is an unwarranted intrusion into this comprehensive regulation.

d. **Dissent** (Marshall, Brennan, Blackmun, Stevens, JJ.). The district court carefully fashioned a remedy based on the evidence before it. The remedy is not prohibited by the Constitution or by the statute and is not an abuse of discretion. The deadline pertains to hearings, not decisions. Since it has been in effect, D has managed to comply in all but one case.

3. **Constitutional Fact and Fundamental Rights.**

a. **Independent judgment.** At one point, the Supreme Court held that in a ratesetting context, if a rate was challenged as confiscatory, a court could exercise its independent judgment in reviewing the agency's determination. [*See* Ohio Valley Water Co. v. Ben Avon Borough, 253 U.S. 287 (1920)] This rule essentially permitted de novo review and has since been discredited. Where an agency decision substantially affects a fundamental vested right, some state courts have exercised their independent judgment as to the evidence. Other state courts disapprove of the independent judgment rule.

**b. Rejection of independent judgment rule--Public Service Commission v. General Telephone Co.,** 555 S.W.2d 395 (Tenn. 1977).

1) **Facts.** The Public Service Commission (D) approved rates that General Telephone Co. (P) considered confiscatory. P appealed to the state courts. The trial court directed D to permit P to earn at least 12% on its common equity, on the ground that any lesser return would be confiscatory. D appeals.

2) **Issue.** In reviewing an agency determination challenged as being confiscatory, may a court apply its independent judgment?

3) **Held.** No. Judgment reversed and remanded.

a) The independent judgment rule was set out in the *Ben Avon* case (*supra*). It has been adopted by the Tennessee courts as well, and has been the standard of review of claims that a rate was confiscatory.

b) Subsequent to the *Ben Avon* case, the Supreme Court has reaffirmed that courts should not substitute their judgment for that of legislative agencies, and that so long as an agency's determination is supported by evidence, it should be upheld. Courts are not to interfere with the ratemaking power unless confiscation is clearly established, which requires proof that the rates are below the lowest limit of the permitted zone of reasonableness.

c) There is a split of authority among the states as to the current validity of the independent judgment rule. Inasmuch as the Supreme Court has abandoned the independent judgment rule, that rule no longer need be followed in Tennessee. The substantial evidence test is constitutionally adequate.

d) Under state law, judicial review is permitted if a decision violates constitutional provisions or is arbitrary or capricious or characterized by abuse of discretion. If a prescribed rate is confiscatory, it will fall within this class of reviewable actions. A reviewing court may evaluate the evidence but may not substitute its judgment for the agency's.

**c. Independent judicial review where fundamental right at stake--Alameda County v. Board of Retirement,** 760 P.2d 464 (Cal. 1988).

1) **Facts.** Carnes applied to the Board of Retirement (D) for a service-connected disability retirement. D conducted hearings and concluded that Carnes was "permanently incapacitated" and should receive the retirement. Alameda County (P) sought a writ of mandate to compel D to set aside its decision. The court held a hearing, independently reviewed and

weighed the evidence in the administrative record, and granted P relief. The court of appeals affirmed. D appeals.

2) **Issue.** When a fundamental right is at stake, should a court exercise independent judicial review when reviewing an agency's adjudicatory decision?

3) **Held.** Yes. Judgment affirmed.

a) The California Code of Civil Procedure provides that a court normally applies a substantial evidence standard in reviewing administrative agency adjudicatory decisions, so that the decision must be upheld if it is supported by substantial evidence. A court may apply the stiffer weight of the evidence standard whenever it is authorized by law to exercise its independent judgment. It is up to the courts to decide which cases warrant the stricter standard of review.

b) The independent judgment test has been applied to cases that threatened to deprive the losing party of a constitutionally protected property right. For example, this property right includes the interest of a private employer in avoiding erroneous charges against its unemployment insurance reserve account.

c) In this case, P is required to participate in its retirement system, and therefore has an interest in protecting the funding of that system. There is no reason to establish a different rule for public employers from that which applies to private employers. Because P faced the loss of a constitutionally protected property right, the court correctly applied the independent judgment test.

4) **Dissent.** The substantial evidence rule is the ordinary rule in the United States. The independent judgment rule is unique and was adopted to protect individual rights against the power of administrative agencies. It does not make sense to allow one government agency such as P to vacate findings of another government agency such as D by just petitioning the court when the legislature has not required P's approval in the first place.

4. ***Chevron* Doctrine.**

a. **Introduction.** Judicial review of an agency's legal rulings is relatively independent, on the theory that the courts can interpret the law as well as an agency. And total deference to agency interpretation would make agencies the final authority on the legality of the use of their own power. Still, the Supreme Court has directed the lower courts to defer to the agencies, even on purely legal issues.

**b.** **Establishment of *Chevron* rule--Chevron v. Natural Resources Defense Council,** 467 U.S. 837 (1984).

1) **Facts.** Amendments to the Clean Air Act required states that had not achieved national air quality standards established by the EPA to create a permit program regulating "major stationary sources" of air pollution. The EPA promulgated a regulation to implement this requirement that allowed a state to interpret the term "stationary source" to include an entire plant as though it were encased within a single "bubble." The National Resources Defense Council (P) challenged the regulation, claiming the term should have been defined to mean every pollution-emitting device, even if there are several within one plant. The Court of Appeals for the District of Columbia Circuit set aside the regulations on the ground that since Congress did not define the term in the statute, the purposes of the nonattainment program should guide interpretation. The court then held that it was inappropriate to apply the bubble concept in programs enacted to improve air quality. The Supreme Court granted certiorari.

2) **Issue.** When an administrative agency has provided a reasonable regulatory interpretation of a term not defined in the underlying statute, may a reviewing court substitute its own interpretation of the same term?

3) **Held.** No. Judgment reversed.

   a) A court reviewing an agency's construction of the statute that it administers faces two questions only: (i) Did Congress manifest its intent? and, if not, (ii) Is the agency's interpretation based on a permissible construction of the statute? *or reasonable*

   b) When Congress explicitly leaves a gap for an agency to fill, it expressly delegates to the agency authority to clarify specific provisions of the statute by regulation. These legislative regulations by the agency are entitled to controlling weight unless they are arbitrary, capricious, or manifestly contrary to the statute. If Congress delegates interpretative authority to an agency in an implicit manner instead of explicitly, then the agency's interpretation must be upheld so long as it is reasonable.

   c) In this case, Congress did not provide any definition of the term "source," but the statutory language suggests that Congress intended to enlarge the scope of the agency's power to regulate particular sources. The legislative history provides no guidance on the definition of the term, either. The parties' policy arguments are better left to legislators or administrators, not judges.

   d) The EPA's interpretation of the term is a reasonable accommodation of the competing interests and the courts must defer to it. If a

*[handwritten margin note: 1) Is congressional intent clear? 2) Agency's reasonable/permissible construction?]*

challenge to an agency's interpretation of a statutory provision is based on the wisdom of the agency's policy, rather than whether it is a reasonable choice within the gap left open by Congress, the challenge must fail. The courts must defer to the agency's policy choices.

Christensen v. Harris

**c.** ***Chevron* deference withheld--Christensen v. Harris,** 529 U.S. 576 (2000).

    **1)** **Facts.** The Fair Labor Standards Act requires that hourly employees be compensated for overtime. Under the Act, states and political subdivisions may compensate their employees for overtime by granting them additional time off with full pay. If the employees do not use the time off, the employer is obligated to pay cash compensation. Concerned that overtime pay claims would bankrupt it, Harris County, Texas, sought an opinion from the Department of Labor's ("DOL's") Wage and Hour Division as to whether it could require nonexempt employees to use their compensatory time. The DOL took the position that it could do so if a "prior agreement specifically provides such a provision." Harris County imposed such a requirement, and several of its employees (Ps) brought suit on grounds that there was no "prior agreement" under the DOL's interpretation. The court of appeals found that nothing in the statute or regulations prohibited an employer from compelling the use of compensatory time.

    **2)** **Issue.** Is the DOL's interpretation consistent with the statute?

    **3)** **Held.** No. Judgment affirmed.

        **a)** *Chevron* provides that a court must give deference to an agency's regulation interpreting an ambiguous statute. The opinion letter at issue here is neither a formal rule nor a formal adjudication subject to notice-and-comment procedures, and does not have the force of law. Moreover, the statute at issue is not ambiguous. The DOL's opinion letter is therefore not entitled to *Chevron* deference.

    **4)** **Concurrence** (Scalia, J.). Under *Chevron*, a court may not substitute its interpretation of a statute for a reasonable interpretation given it by the administrator of an agency. In fact, *Chevron* involved an interpretive regulation. *Chevron* deference has been accorded not only to formal rulemaking, but in a number of other contexts. However, the DOL's interpretation of the statute in this case was not reasonable.

National Fuel Gas Supply Corp. v. FERC

**d.** **Deference to agency's legal interpretation of settlement agreement--National Fuel Gas Supply Corp. v. FERC,** 811 F.2d 1563 (D.C. Cir. 1987).

    **1)** **Facts.** The National Fuel Gas Supply Corp. (P) applied to the Federal Energy Regulatory Commission (D) for a retroactive rate increase for selling natural gas in interstate commerce. P's application was based on a reversal by the Supreme Court of D's regulation that prohibited pricing at higher "first sale gas" levels for gas produced and sold by a single company. D denied P's application for one period of time (Period I) because P's rates had been fixed in a final adjudication before D that addressed all of the issues P raised. As for Period II, D denied retroactive adjustments because P's rates had been established in a settlement reached with its customers and approved in an order entered by D. The settlement order failed to preserve any right for P to object to these rates later on the ground that the gas had been priced improperly under the Act. P appeals.

2) **Issue.** Must a court defer to an agency's interpretation of a settlement agreement the agency reached with a private company it regulates?

3) **Held.** Yes. Judgment affirmed.

    a)    D correctly denied P's application with respect to the Period I.

    b)    The issue regarding Period II is whether the settlement agreement either reserved the issue or simply did not cover the issue. D interpreted the agreement to address the issue of whether to value P's own gas production on a cost-of-service basis, and that P did not reserve the right to reprise this gas if it were later found to be "first sale" gas under the Act.

    c)    There are two possible approaches to this issue. The court could either give no deference to D's reading on the ground that a court may freely review an agency's holding on a ruling of law, or the court could defer even on matters of pure legal interpretation. Under *Chevron*, the correct view requires a court to give deference, even when the issue is simply the proper construction of language.

    d)    *Chevron* involved an implicit delegation of power to the agency. The delegation of adjudicative authority is explicit. Congress has delegated to D a broad range of adjudicative powers over natural gas rates. Such an explicit delegation of power compels the courts to defer to the agency's conclusions even on "pure" questions of law within the agency's domain.

    e)    Regardless of *Chevron*, deference is appropriate because the congressional grant of authority to the agency indicates that the agency's interpretation typically will be enhanced by the agency's technical knowledge, even when the agency is simply interpreting a legal document. In this case, Congress by statute required D to take an active role in approving the settlement agreement. In deciding to approve the agreement, D had to construe its provisions, and this is another reason for deference.

**e.   Government subsidies to speech--Rust v. Sullivan,** 500 U.S. 173 (1991).

    **1)   Facts.** Congress enacted Title X of the Public Health Service Act that provided federal funding for family-planning services, provided that none of the funds could be used in programs where abortion is a method of family planning. Sullivan (D), Secretary of the Department of Health and Human Services, promulgated new regulations that (i) specified that a Title X project cannot provide counseling concerning abortion or referrals for abortion; (ii) prohibited a Title X project from engaging in activities that encourage, promote, or advocate abortion as a method of family planning; and (iii) required that Title X projects be physically and financially separate from prohibited abortion activities. Rust and others (Ps) challenged the facial validity of the regulations, claiming they violated First and Fifth Amendments to the Constitution. The lower courts upheld the regulations. The Supreme Court granted certiorari.

    **2)   Issue.** May the federal government condition the acceptance of federal funds by a particular project on the project's agreement to refrain from promoting or even discussing abortion?

    **3)   Held.** Yes. Judgment affirmed.

        a)   D's regulations do not exceed D's authority so long as they reflect a plausible construction of the plain language of the statute and do not otherwise conflict with Congress's expressed intent. The language of the statute is ambiguous and broad enough to allow D's interpretation. Courts normally must defer to the expertise of the agency charged with administering the law. The fact that the regulations are a change from the prior regulations is justified by D's experience under the prior policy.

        b)   Ps are claiming that the regulations are discrimination based on viewpoint because they promote childbirth over abortion. But D has merely chosen to fund one activity to the exclusion of the other. The government has no obligation to subsidize counterpart rights once it decides to subsidize one protected right. D's regulations do not deny anyone a benefit, but merely require that public funds be spent for the purposes for which they were authorized. And they apply to the project, not to the grantee, who is left free to perform abortions and to advocate abortion in other contexts.

        c)   Ps also claim that D's regulations violate a woman's Fifth Amendment right to choose whether to terminate her pregnancy. But Congress's refusal to fund abortion counseling and advocacy leaves a pregnant woman with the same choices as if Congress had chosen not to fund family-planning services at all. D's regulations do not affect a doctor's ability to provide information about abortion outside the context of a Title X project.

**4)** **Comment.** The Court noted that government funding is not always sufficient by itself to justify government control over the content of expression. For example, government ownership of real property does not justify restriction of speech in such areas if they have been traditionally open to the public for expressive activity, and government payments to universities do not justify control of speech there. In this case, D's regulations do not significantly impinge upon the doctor-patient relationship because they do not apply to post-conception medical care, and the doctor can make it clear that advice regarding abortion is beyond the scope of the Title X program.

**f.** **Congressional intent--Food and Drug Administration v. Brown & Williamson Tobacco Corp.,** 529 U.S. 120 (2000).

**1)** **Facts.** The Food and Drug Administration ("FDA") promulgated regulations under the Food, Drug and Cosmetic Act ("FDCA") intended to reduce tobacco consumption among children and adolescents. Tobacco companies, retailers, and advertisers (Ps) objected on grounds that the FDA held no jurisdiction to regulate tobacco. The court of appeals agreed with Ps and the Supreme Court granted certiorari.

**2)** **Issue.** Does the FDA have statutory authority to regulate tobacco?

**3)** **Held.** No. Judgment affirmed.

 a) Where Congress has specifically addressed a question, *Chevron* deference of the agency's interpretation is not appropriate. Where Congress has directly spoken to the precise question at issue, the court must give effect to the unambiguously expressed Congressional intent.

 b) In interpreting a statute, it must be read in its context and with a view to its place in the overall statutory scheme.

 c) The FDCA seeks to assure that any produce regulated by the FDA is safe and effective for its intended use. The FDA has concluded that tobacco is unsafe. Under the statute, therefore, if the FDA has jurisdiction over tobacco, it must ban its sale in interstate commerce.

 d) But Congress has addressed tobacco in legislation on numerous occasions. Its decision to regulate labeling and advertising of tobacco reveals its intention not to ban the sale of tobacco. A ban on the sale of tobacco by the FDA would contravene Congressional policy. Congress therefore must have intended to put tobacco beyond the reach of the FDCA. Therefore, the FDA lacks jurisdiction to regulate tobacco.

**4)** **Dissent** (Breyer, Stevens, Souter, Ginsburg, JJ.). Tobacco falls within the literal language of the FDCA. Moreover, the principal purpose of the FDCA—to protect public health—supports the proposition that tobacco falls within it. Therefore, the FDA has jurisdiction to regulate tobacco.

# TABLE OF CASES
(Page numbers of briefed cases in bold)

# NOTES

Up to e̅ individual to decide e̅ amt of deference to give to experts.

# NOTES

# NOTES

# NOTES

# NOTES

# NOTES

# NOTES

# NOTES

# NOTES

TYPICAL PROCEDURE FOR CONTESTED CASES (ADJUDICATION) PROCEEDING

1. Application is filed w/ ē MPSC (Commission)

2. Case is assigned a Staff Case Coordinator (Internal Procedure)

3. Commission's Executive Secretary reviews & sets in conjunction w/ ALJ division a prehearing date & issues a notice of hearing.

4. Chief ALJ assigns ē case to an ALJ

5. Prehearing is held. A schedule for ē remainder of ē case is set.

6. Hearing is held b/4 an ALJ.

7. ALJ issues Proposal for Decision (PFD) containing findings of facts & interpretations of laws/rules

8. Exceptions & replies to exceptions are filed.

9. Record, exceptions & replies to exceptions are transmitted to ē Commission

10. Commission issues its orders which is subj. to appeal by ē pty for judicial review.

# NOTES

# NOTES

inferior officer = pg 38 + 39

pg 692 = exhaustion